Windmills of England

Windmills of England

by

R. J. BROWN

ROBERT HALE · LONDON

ISBN 0 7091 5641 3

Robert Hale & Company
Clerkenwell House
Clerkenwell Green
London EC1R 0HT

Photoset, printed and bound
in Great Britain by
REDWOOD BURN LIMITED
Trowbridge & Esher

Contents

OTHER PRESERVED OR OUTSTANDING MILLS

Acknowledgements

During the research carried out in the preparation of this book, I am indebted to the various people who have assisted me. In particular I would like to thank my wife for her encouragement and assistance throughout and also to my three children, David, Katherine and Peter for their help and particularly David who photographed most of the mills.

I would also like to express my appreciation for the help and co-operation I have received from numerous public bodies, in particular the staff of the following Public Libraries: Birmingham, Blackpool, Brighton, Cambridge, Canterbury, Chester, Colchester, Derby, Grimsby, Hull, Ipswich, Lincoln, Lytham, Norwich, Southend, Sunderland, Taunton; and also to the staff of the following Record Offices: Cambridgeshire, East Sussex, Essex, Hertfordshire, Kent, Norfolk, Suffolk, Warwickshire.

PART ONE

Windmills–Their Design, Machinery and Workings

ORIGIN AND DECLINE

The first appearance of the windmill in this country is lost in history and as to whether they were an imported idea or the product of natural development is now uncertain. One theory is that they originated in the Middle East, being brought back by the Crusaders; others that they were discovered in China, or that they were developed in Europe. It is known that no windmills were recorded in the Domesday Book, for the mills referred to in that document were either water or horse mills. The earliest authentic reference to a windmill dates from 1185, when a windmill in the village of Weedley, Yorkshire, was let at a rent of 8s. per year.

The earliest illustration of a post mill is contained in the English Windmill Psalter, believed to have been written about 1260. The manuscript was purchased in 1896 by William Morris and is now housed in the Pierpont Morgan Library in New York. Another excellent illustration of a post mill is on a memorial brass in St Margaret's Church, Kings Lynn, which commemorates a Mayor of the town, Adam de Walsoken, who died of the Black Death in 1348. The earliest illustration of a tower mill is depicted in an illuminated manuscript prepared in 1420 in France of the Porter family of England. Windmills, commonly regarded as part of the everyday landscape, are to be found on numerous medieval manuscripts, carvings, stained glasswork and brasses.

From the thirteenth century onwards windmills spread throughout England, and even into North Wales and Scotland, until at one time as many as ten thousand were at work in England. The corn mills were more numerous in the fairly flat corn-growing counties of Kent, Sussex, Surrey, Essex, Suffolk, Cambridgeshire, Norfolk, Lincolnshire and the East Midlands where water power was lacking. Other areas were in the Lancashire Fylde, Cheshire and Anglesey—the granary of Wales. In the Western counties, where there are many streams, there were few windmills, although Somerset had a reasonable number. Drainage mills were restricted generally to the area of the Fens and Broads with, at one time, over two thousand mills draining the Fens alone.

At the end of the nineteenth century the decline of the corn mill began at a time when the design of the windmill was at its peak. The reasons for this was mainly the introduction of the steam mills at the large ports, which ground large quantities of foreign grain, but the depression in agriculture, the depopulation of the countryside and the improvement of transport, enabling flour to be sent to all areas with ease, all added to their disappearance. The decline was accelerated during and after the First World War when, due to government regulations, many millers were forced to grind animal feed only. The number of working mills reduced from about three hundred and fifty in 1919 to about fifty in 1946. During this period the elements destroyed many derelict mills, the post and smock mills being most vulnerable, but also many brick and stone tower mills were pulled down when their materials were required for re-use elsewhere. After the Second World War the lack of materials caused the demolition of several other mills that might have been preserved.

Drainage mills, like the corn mills, were superseded first by steam and later by oil and electric pumps and, although mills on the Broads were built as late as 1912, their decline was rapid and by the 1950s all mills had stopped pumping.

PRESERVATION

The first mill to be preserved was in 1883, when the mill on Wimbledon Common was restored by public subscription, and in 1894 the tower mill at Bidston, Merseyside, was preserved by Mr Hudson, of soap fame. In 1929 a greater effort was made and the Society for the Protection of Ancient Buildings began to take an interest in windmills, with the result that by 1931 a Windmill Section of the Society was formed. The Windmill Section was continuously short of money, but much good work was carried out. However, the Second World War and the shortage of materials after the war temporarily halted the Society's progress.

Over the last twenty-five years a great amount of work has been carried out on the restoration of windmills, with financial assistance from local and county councils. Many mills have been restored by local groups of enthusiasts, raising the money and carrying out the work themselves. In the 1950s many mills were restored, but unfortunately some of these were concerned mainly with the outward appearance of the mill, with the machinery being removed, so these were only shell restorations. In the 1960s and 1970s a greater effort was made to restore mills to their original condition. Some, although no longer in working order and having only skeleton sails and fantail to lessen the wind pressure, are completely restored internally. Many mills have, however, been restored to working order. Fine examples are the post mill at Wrawby, Humberside, which was rebuilt after the mill had been virtually dismantled, and the post mill at Nutley, Sussex.

POST MILLS

The earliest windmills in this country were post mills, deriving their name from the great post on which the body, containing the machinery, turns to face the wind. The appearance of medieval windmills can be seen from the many representations that have survived and they differed little from the mills of centuries later.

The body of the mill was carried and pivoted on a massive central post, called the 'main post', about which the body of the mill revolved. Oak was generally used for the main post, but at Clayton, Argos Hill and Blackboys post mills, all in Sussex, four pieces of pitch pine clamped and pegged together were used. Supporting the main post were four raking 'quarterbars' each morticed into the main post at one end and the other end generally framed to the 'crosstrees' by means of a birdsmouth joint and iron straps. The main post was quartered over the crosstrees, but was not supported by them, being kept an inch or two above them. These crosstrees were first laid directly on or buried beneath the surface of the ground to give the mill greater stability. Later they were raised on brick piers but not fixed to them. Nearly all medieval post mills appear to have been sunken mills, for out of the eight examples of medieval windmill sites described in John Salmon's *The Windmill in English Medieval Art*, all had traces of crosstrees buried in the ground. Most post mills were constructed with two crosstrees set at right angles to each other, but a few mills had three crosstrees and six quarterbars. These were at Chinnor and Stokenchurch both in Oxfordshire, Bledlow Ridge, Buckinghamshire, Costock, Nottinghamshire and Moreton, Essex. All of these have now either collapsed or been demolished, the last to disappear being Moreton Mill which was demolished in 1965.

The top of the post terminated either with a 'pintle', turned out of the solid, or an iron gudgeon or 'Sampson head'—a cap and bearing of iron. Pivoting and rotating on top of this was a great transverse beam, called the 'crowntree', on which the weight of the body of the mill rested. The framing of the mill varied greatly. Generally, on each end of the crowntree, were fixed the 'side girts' which were morticed and dowelled, with hardwood trenails, to the four corner posts. About these timbers the mill was formed; the top and bottom side girts, at the eaves and the lower ground floor, ran parallel to the side girts and between these were vertical studs with diagonal bracings. At the breast and tail, cross timbers, called the 'breast' and 'tail beams', were secured to the top side girts to carry the neck and tail bearings of the windshaft respectively. In addition the breast beam was supported in its centre by a vertical member, called the 'prick-post'. The breast beam was sometimes curved, while others were splayed to form an obtuse angle at the centre and, occasionally, others were set forward with the top side girts extended to support the beam. Two large horizontal timbers, called 'sheers', were fixed either side of the main post, the full length of the body and beneath the lower floor, to support the mill about the post. Beneath these was a 'collar' or 'girdle'—a heavy wooden frame around the main-post—which steadied the mill in rough weather, relieving the strain from the main-post. Occasionally other methods have been used to steady the mill: at Sprowston Mill, Norwich, a ball-bearing collar was used and this is now at The Bridewell Museum, Norwich. At Argos Hill, Sussex, a vertical iron track was fitted round the main-post and iron rollers on brackets fixed to the underside of the lower floor.

Early mills had a simple pitched roof, as at Bourn, Cambridgeshire, but later curved rafters were generally used to accommodate the larger brake wheel. At Cromer Mill, Hertfordshire, an ogee roof can be seen, the rafters being shaped to follow a reverse curve to a point at the ridge. The whole of the framing was usually covered by horizontal shiplap boarding either painted white or tarred, but some post mills in Yorkshire were covered with vertical boarding, while in Sussex mills were occasionally partly or almost completely covered with flat galvanized iron sheets painted white. The post mills at Argos Hill and Clayton are clad on the breast only, but the mill at Cross-in-Hand has the breast and sides clad. To make the mill waterproof the boarding to the breast was extended beyond the sides, with the sides and the roof carried beyond the rear boarding. A number of mills had the weatherboard to the breast carried down below the lower floor in a shield-like extension, as at Chillenden Mill, Kent, to give protection to the sub-structure of the mill. Some mills had the weatherboarding lath-and-plastered inside to keep the interior dry and free from draughts. At Aythorpe Roding, Essex, the interior of the roof, with part of the walls of the floor below, was similarly treated.

Access to the mill body was gained by means of a wide ladder from the ground up to the platform at the rear of the lower floor. Above this ladder many mills had a porch canopy over the door and this varied greatly from mill to mill. Some had a simple lean-to, some a pitched roof, some a flat curve, while others were bonnet shaped. In Norfolk and West Suffolk many mills had full-width porches and were sometimes completely enclosed. Some post mills had balconies at the rear, as at Holton, Suffolk, and a few even had galleries round the eaves.

The early post mills were the open-trestle type, but in the late eighteenth and early nineteenth centuries roundhouses were added to give protection to the substructure and to provide extra storage space. These roundhouses were not attached to the mill in any way, the main-post passing through an opening at the apex of the roof. Later, many mills in East Suffolk had the roundhouse built at the same time as the mill itself, and some had as many as three floors and were as high as the body of the mill proper. Mills were sometimes raised when the roundhouse was constructed and the mill at Saxtead Green was raised three times altogether, the last time probably in 1854. The roundhouse at Holton, Suffolk, has two floors, one of which is below ground level. The walls were generally built of brick, stone or flint, but in Sussex timber walls were sometimes used. The roofs were almost always boarded and felted, but a few had tiles—as at Stevington Mill, Bedfordshire—slates and even thatch. The weatherboarding of the mill body was extended down and shaped to clear the roof of the roundhouse. Some mills had a small petticoat, attached to the underside of the lower floor of the mill, to protect the opening in the roof of the roundhouse. Occasionally the roundhouse had no roof and in this case the petticoat was built out to form the top of the roundhouse. Two doors were provided, on opposite sides of the roundhouse, so that access could be obtained wherever the sails were positioned.

In the Midland-type post mill the roundhouse roof was attached to the body of the mill with support gained by timbers set at right angles to the sheers, called 'outriggers'. Cast-iron rollers were fitted to the ends of the sheers and outriggers which ran on a curb on top of the roundhouse wall. This arrangement can be seen at Cat and Fiddle Mill, Dale Abbey, Derbyshire.

Medieval mills had only one pair of stones situated in the breast. Later two stones were used—one in the breast and the other in the tail—the breast stone being driven direct from the brake wheel, while the stone in the tail was driven by an additional tail wheel. The body of the early mills were often extended at the rear to accommodate the extra stone; this can be seen at Bourn Mill, Cambridgeshire, where false corner posts were provided. In East Anglia the large post mills often drove two stones in the breast, while others had an additional stone in the tail and a few had four stones—two in the breast and two in the tail.

Most post mills were not designed to accommodate the bolters, wire machines, jumpers and oat crushers, but many mills incorporated some of these machines. Generally this machinery was fitted in the tail of the mill, but in Lancashire the body had compartments built out from the side of the mill to house the additional machinery. This can be seen from old photographs of Formby Mill which was pulled down in 1884.

TOWER MILLS

The tower mill was a logical development from the post mill. It consisted of a fixed tower built of stone or brickwork with a timber cap, which contained the windshaft—the cap being the only part which turned to face the wind. The oldest recorded tower mill in England was one at Dover Castle dated 1295, while the oldest surviving tower mill is at Burton Dasset, Warwickshire, which has for years been called 'The Beacon', but was, according to a fifteenth-century deed, actually built as a tower mill.

The early tower mill was short with a conical cap and, with the windshaft mounted horizontally, the tower had to be cylindrical in shape in order that the sails could clear the face of the tower. An example of this type of tower can be seen at Portland Bill, Dorset. The towers were usually two or three floors enabling the common sails to be set by hand from the ground and the cap turned into the wind by means of a tail pole. Later, when the windshafts were inclined, the towers were built with a batter giving the mill greater stability and allowing more room at the base where space was needed. The smaller cap also gave better airflow behind the sails. Most towers were round, but sometimes they were polygonal and occasionally they varied in shape as the tower increased in height. The derelict mill at Lutton Gowts, Lincolnshire, built in 1746, is octagonal while a mill at Kenninghall, Norfolk, was ten-sided becoming round half way up. Gibraltar Mill, Great Bardfield, Essex, is even more unusual, being octagonal at the base with chamfered corners, sixteen-sided half way up and round at the top. The towers were built of local materials—generally brick in the South and East and stone in the North and West—and were often tarred, rendered, painted or occasionally even tile hung, as at Halnaker Mill, Sussex, to protect them against the weather.

Most tower mills had five or six floors, but some had as little as three, while the great tower mill at Southtown, Great Yarmouth, Norfolk, had as many as twelve. The mill, which was built in 1812 for a cost of £10,000, was badly damaged in a severe storm in 1894 and was sold at auction for £100 in 1904. Demolished the following year, the bricks were re-used to build a row of cottages, known as Mill Cottages, which still exist. This mill was the largest ever built in Europe being 122 feet high to top of the cap and 40 feet diameter at the base of the tower. Generally the taller tower mills were not built until the introduction of the patent sail and then many were built with a stage at first or second floor enabling the miller to adjust the sails from the stage.

Tower mills were sometimes raised; the mill at Arkley, London Borough of Barnet, was raised a few courses while North Leverton Mill, Nottinghamshire, has been raised one floor.

SMOCK MILLS
A variation of the tower mill was the smock mill, which derived its name from its likeness to the linen smock that was once the traditional dress of the British countryman. The smock mill was, in fact, a tapering, timber tower covered with weatherboarding. Generally they were octagonal in shape but six, ten, twelve-sided smocks have been constructed. Most smock mills were built on a brick base which was sometimes only a few courses high, as at Stelling Minnis, Kent, but generally comprised one, two or even three floors.

The main structural framing of a smock mill were the large timber corner or 'cant' posts at each corner, which extended for the full height and converged to give the body of the mill its batter. These cant posts

18

were secured to timber wall plates or sills which were bedded on top of the brick base. The inherent weakness was that it was difficult to provide a satisfactory fixing between the cant post and the sill and there was a natural tendency for the feet of the cant posts to move outwards allowing the structure to collapse. The cant posts were sometimes secured with iron straps bolted to oak blocks on the inside of the sills, while occasionally the posts were mounted on iron shoes bolted to the sill. At the top, the cant posts were framed into the timber track or curb on which the cap rotated. Between each cant post were horizontal ledges, housed at each end to these posts, with a vertical central post fixed between the ledges, strengthened with diagonal braces and filled in with vertical studs to ensure a strong and stable structure. Two large beams, called 'binders', carried each floor and these were partly framed into the cant post and rested on the horizontal ledges. These binders were arranged at right angles to those of the floor above, so spreading the load around the mill.

The smock mill was generally covered by horizontal weatherboarding, but in Cambridgeshire vertical boarding was sometimes used and can still be seen at the derelict mills at Swaffham Prior and Sawtry. At West Wratting Mill, Cambridgeshire, the sides were horizontally boarded and overlaid with vertical boards on four sides. The corners were always vulnerable and to overcome this problem alternate horizontal boards to each side were extended over the adjoining boards of the other side. These corners were protected by a strip of lead or zinc to make them weatherproof. The boarding of the smock mill, like the post mill, was either tarred or painted white.

Like the tower mill the taller smock mills had a stage, usually fixed to the brick base at the first floor or the meal floor, so the miller could load up the grist wagon or regulate the sails with ease. These stages were generally of wood, but sometimes of iron and a few a combination of both. They were supported by brackets out from the brick base, but the odd stage, usually in Kent, was supported by vertical uprights. Two doors were provided onto the stage, opposite each other, so access could be obtained no matter where the sails were positioned and this also applied to the doors on the ground floor whether the mill had a stage or not. Occasionally a gallery was fixed around the cap, but this was most uncommon on a smock mill. The smock mill, like the brick tower mill, varied greatly in size from several floors, as at Cranbrook, Kent, to a few floors, as at West Wratting, Cambridgeshire.

COMPOSITE MILLS

The composite mill was a combination of a post mill and tower mill. The mill had the body of a post mill with the post removed and mounted on a short tower, in the same way as a cap, which ran on castors or tram-wheels. The whole body was turned into the wind by a tail pole or a fan-tail mounted on the roof with the drive taken down to the curb on the tower. There were only a few of these mills built and, with the exception of the one built at Monk Soham, Suffolk, were all adaptions and the only advantage seems to be that of economy—using a sound body of a post mill rather than having it demolished.

HOLLOW POST MILLS

An unusual design was the hollow post mill, a Dutch invention, which was first used for drainage. It had a small post-mill type body, which contained the windshaft, brake wheel and wallower, and an upright shaft which passed down through a hollow post to drive the machinery below. Only a few of these mills were built in England, the most famous being the mill at Wimbledon Common built as a hollow post mill in 1817, but later rebuilt as a composite.

A variation was the small, skeleton, hollow post mill often used for drainage and these were very numerous in the Fens and the Norfolk Broads. These windpumps were skeleton framed, winded by a large weather vane and driving the pump, by common sails, through a crank in the windshaft. Although none now survive in the Fens or Broads there are two examples still to be found in Kent, at Stodmarsh and Iwade.

HORIZONTAL MILLS

Horizontal mills were introduced in this country by Captain Stephen Hooper, who erected the first on his property at Margate, Kent, at the end of the eighteenth century and continued to work it until about 1830 when she was damaged in a storm. In 1788 another horizontal mill was erected at Battersea to Hooper's design, but the upkeep and repairs were extremely high and she fell into disrepair before being finally demolished in 1849 when Battersea Park was laid out.

The general design was that of a tall tower divided into two parts, the machinery contained in the lower part while the upper part had a large paddle wheel, which revolved in a horizontal plane, some 40 feet in diameter and 28 feet high. Around the paddle wheel were fitted vertical slats which could be turned on their axes thus directing the wind and activating the paddle wheel. The wheel was fixed to the upright shaft driving the stones on the lower floors in the usual way.

DRAINAGE MILLS

Windmills were not used only for grinding corn or other cereals. Many were used in the grinding of snuff, pepper, mustard and vegetable oil, but by far the greatest additional function of the windmill was its use in the drainage of land, and many mills were used for this purpose on the Fens and the Norfolk Broads.

The drainage of the Fens commenced in the sixteenth century and the earliest mill recorded was at Holbeach, Lincolnshire, in 1588. The number steadily increased until the introduction of steam pumps at the beginning of the nineteenth century and these, together with the drying out and shrinkage of the soil, slowly put an end to the mills. These mills were generally smock mills and except for the small mill at Wicken Fen, the nature reserve, and a few remains elsewhere, all these mills have now disappeared.

The mills on the Norfolk Broads are more numerous and many derelict mills remain today, for these were generally brick built, sometimes tarred, with a typical boat-shaped boarded cap. These mills were built as late as 1914 and the last one to work by wind was at Ashtree Farm, which finally ceased work at the beginning of 1953 when part of the windshaft and sails were blown off. Some fine drainage mills remain today, being restored over the last twenty years, and those at Stracey Arms, Thurne Dyke, Horsey Mere and Berney Arms are excellent examples. It was a lonely existence, for many mills were in remote, isolated positions and were sometimes only accessible by water and the marshmen often lived with their families in these mills. In many instances these brick towers replaced earlier smock mills, the only one to survive is at Herringfleet, Suffolk, on the River Waveney.

Internally the machinery was very simple with the brake wheel driving the wallower mounted on the upright shaft which rotated and drove at ground level, an inverted bevel gear. This gear engaged the 'pit wheel', which in turn drove a shaft that passed outside the mill onto which was mounted the 'paddle' or 'scoop wheel'. This generally consisted of a central iron frame carrying wooden blades and these were enclosed by a wooden semi-circular casing or 'hoodway' against the side of the mill. As these paddles revolved the water was scooped up, discharging it at a higher level. The scoop wheels varied greatly in size, depending on the power of the mill and also the design of the wheel. Later mills often employed the Appold turbine which was up to fifty per cent more efficient than a scoop wheel.

REMOVALS

Post and smock mills were never regarded as permanent structures and there were many occasions when these were moved to new sites. Post mills had the machinery removed and the body of the mill moved, either on rollers or purpose made sledges, to the new position by up to several dozen oxen or horses. Several post mills were moved on more than one occasion. Smock mills were either sawn down each cant post and moved in sections, or completely dismantled with each member numbered, or the whole body carried on carts while the machinery and cap were transported separately. It was not only post and smock mills that were moved,

21

for tower mills too were also moved, but in these cases only the machinery, sails and cap were removed being fitted into a new tower built in the new location.

CONVERSION OF MILLS TO DWELLINGS

Over the last fifty years many old tower mills, and some smock mills, have been converted into dwellings. Many excellent examples exist throughout the country; those at Cley-next-Sea, Burnham Overy and Weybourne, Norfolk, Great Bardfield, Essex and Morcott, Leicestershire, being some of the finest. These, and some others, hardly detract from the outward appearance of the mills, for all are complete with mock sails and fantails. Unfortunately not all mills are converted in a sympathetic manner. Like oast houses and barns a very special approach is required if the character of the structure is to remain.

SAILS

Early sails were formed of a simple wooden framework, consisting of a number of horizontal bars or 'sail bars', evenly spaced and morticed through a timber 'whip' and joined together along each side to a longitudinal batten, called a 'hemlath'. Two heavier timbers, called 'stocks', were set at right angles, morticed through the end of the windshaft and wedged in position, onto which the sails were bolted and strapped. Each sail was spread with canvas being threaded in and out of the bars and drawn towards the whip from the hemlaths. These sails formed a flat plane and were set at a constant angle to the windshaft.

Later these sails were replaced by common sails. These comprised a lattice-like framework with the sail area only to the driving side of the whip. A narrow 'leading board', inclined at an angle, was attached to the driving side of the sail to assist the flow of wind to the canvas. A further improvement was to give the sail an 'angle of weather'—a twist similar to that of a propeller. At the inner end of the sail frame was an iron rod, the full width of the sail, onto which the canvas was attached by means of rings and eyelets, with the rings corded. These cords run down both sides of the sails, enabling the sail to be spread over the sail and fastened at the bottom. The sail cloth was spread across the face of the sail and not threaded in and out of the sail bars as the earlier cloths had been. Additional cords, called 'pointing lines', were attached to the edge of the canvas, enabling the miller to reef his sails to suit the strength of the wind—from a narrow triangle of canvas, called 'sword point', and onto 'dagger point', 'first reef' and 'full sail'. When the mill was at rest the canvas was wound up and hooked over the timber 'sail cleats' on the whip. The common sail had one great disadvantage; when the wind strength changed the area of sail could not be adjusted without first stopping the mill, and it was then necessary to bring each sail to its lowest

22

position in turn. This was often an arduous, dangerous operation, especially in stormy or wet weather, and accidents sometimes occurred when the sails moved because of inadequate braking.

In 1772 Andrew Meikle, a Scottish millwright, introduced the spring sail—a sail designed to 'spill the wind' during squalls and storms. The canvas was substituted by a number of small, rectangular, hinged shutters. All the shutters in a sail were connected together by a wooden 'shutter bar', running the full length of the sail, which in turn was connected by a lever to a iron rod controlled by a coil or an elliptic leaf spring, that kept the shutters closed against normal wind pressure, but if the pressure increased beyond a safe limit the shutters would open. The spring sail also had disadvantages. It was less powerful than the common sail and it was not unusual to use two common sails in conjunction with two spring sails. This gave a reasonable amount of power with a certain degree of self-regulating control. The sails still had to be stopped by the brake and the springs initially tensioned by means of an iron rod and lever at the end of each sail. Also the shutters had a tendency to move during each revolution, opening at the top and closing at the bottom, and as each sail came in front of the mill, the shutters 'snapped', spraying water, in wet weather, onto the breast of the mill.

A variation of the spring sail was invented, in 1789, by Captain Stephen Hooper. This was the roller reefing sail, which replaced the shutters of the ordinary spring sail with a number of small roller blinds. The top of each blind was fastened to the bottom of the blind above it by two webbing straps called 'listings'. Two shutter bars, one at each end of the blinds, ran the length of the sail and were operated by two diagonal wooden rods called 'air poles'. These were connected, at the front of the windshaft, by a series of cranks and levers to a spider coupling which, in turn, was connected to a striking rod that passed through the centre of the hollow windshaft. At the end of the striking rod was a rack engaging with a pinion on the spindle of the chain wheel. Attached to the wheel was a endless chain which passed down to the ground. By pulling the chain the striking rod moved backwards and forwards thus rolling or unrolling the blinds. It was, therefore, possible to alter the amount of sail according to the power required without first stopping the mill. This system gained some popularity especially in Yorkshire, but it was not regarded as being efficient as the listings were apt to break. In 1804 William Bywaters of Nottingham took out a patent on a different type of roller reefing sail, this had rollers parallel to the sail stocks, but this was not very successful and few appear to have been used.

The next development and by far the most important in sail design, came about in 1807 when Sir William Cubitt devised his 'patent sail'. For this he combined the shutters of the spring sail with the control of the roller reefing sail. There was only one shutter bar to each sail, similar to the spring sail, controlling each shutter and attached at the top to the 'bell-cranks' or 'triangles' which, in turn, was connected to the central spider projecting from the windshaft. The gearing between the spider and the chain wheel was similar to the roller reefing system, but weights were suspended from the endless chain. These weights would keep the shutters closed until, as the wind pressure increased, it overcame the weights and the shutters opened. This could be achieved on all sails without stopping the mill.

Striking rods also ended, by various means, with a 'rocking lever'. The chain was attached from the end of this lever, hung down to the ground, up again to the fantail where it passed over a pulley in a bar fixed to the fan frame and down to the lever. Weights were again attached to the end of the chain.

There were many variations to shuttered sails; both single and double were used extensively—the single sail having its working surface on one side of the whip only, while the double sail had its working surface on both sides. Generally it was regarded that single-shuttered sails, each with a light leading board, were more efficient in light winds than double-shuttered sails. Shuttered sails varied greatly in size, varying in width from 6 to 10 feet, with the width of the shutters varying between 7 and 12 inches and 1 to 6 feet in length. A variation to the double-shuttered sail was used in Kent and Sussex. These sails had a narrow leading side, the outer part carried shutters while the inner part was fixed with a wide leading board called a 'dead lead'.

Another form of sail was the spring-patent sail which was a combination of the spring and patent sail. At Patcham, Barnham, Clayton and Medmerry tower mills, all in Sussex, the arm of the spider coupling consisted of a two-leaf spring, while at Outwood smock mill a double half-elliptic spring was fitted between the bell crank and the shutter bar of each sail. Two Essex mills—Little Laver and High Easter—had laminated spring spiders, half elliptic but not inverted as at Patcham. This form of spring sail combined the advantage of individual spring sails in smoothing out the running of the mill in gusty weather, with the advantage of patent sails in control of the sails simultaneously.

Several mills in Suffolk were fitted with an air brake, known as 'sky-scrapers'. The device was invented by Robert Catchpole, a millwright from Sudbury, Suffolk, and consisted of two longitudinal shutters fixed side by side on the outer end of the leading edge of each sail, and controlled by the same mechanism which operated the main shutters. The object was to give additional sail area in fair winds, but in high winds the shutters opened causing them to act as a brake. The tower mill at Buxhall, and the post mills at Drinkstone, Gedding and Wetherden were fitted with this device. In Yorkshire, at Tollerton and Hessle Mills, air brakes were provided by inserting two longitudinal shutters, end to end, in the leading boards of roller reefing sails.

The frame of a shuttered sail consisted of a number of sail bars, usually eight or ten, spaced approximately three feet apart forming a series of bays. To each bay the shutters were fitted, generally three per bay, but the number varied and in the Fylde and the Wirral Peninsula one shutter per bay was common. The shutter bars were fixed to the hemlath and each sail bar was braced at the back by 'backstays' from the whip to the hemlath. The shutters were of either wood, or framed in stout wire or wood and covered with painted canvas. Each shutter was hinged by means of a pivoted casting, with one end having an iron lever coupled to the shutter bar enabling the complete set of shutters to be operated simultaneously. In the North-west the sails tapered and the width at the inner end could be 2 feet 6 inches wider than that at the tip. In the case of patent sails all the shutters were, therefore, of different lengths.

Another form of sail was the annular or circular sail which was fitted on four mills in East Anglia. A tower mill at Haverhill, Suffolk, was the first to be built in 1860. It contained a vast wheel, 50 feet in diameter, instead of sails, with 120 patent controlled shutters, 5 feet long and tapering from $12\frac{1}{2}$ to 14 inches wide. A smock mill at Boxford, Suffolk, and post mills at Roxwell, Essex, and at Feltwell, Norfolk, also employed annular sails. All these mills have now been demolished.

Not all mills use four sails—some mills being driven with five, six or eight sails—and in all sixty or seventy multi-sailed mills were built in England, of which over half were built in Lincolnshire. It is generally considered that John Smeaton, the great engineer who built Eddystone Lighthouse, introduced the first multi-sailed mill at Leeds in 1774, but there are earlier references. In the manorial accounts of Framlingham, Suffolk, for the year 1279 there is reference to a 'six-sailed mill', while it is known that six sails were fitted to a post mill at Little Crosby, Merseyside, in 1709. The purpose of a multi-sailed mill was to increase the sail area thus providing greater power. This could have been obtained by increasing the size of the four sails, but the extra weight of the sail would have presented many difficulties. The five-sailed mill was probably the most efficient, but its disadvantage was that the loss of one sail would upset the balance of the sails, putting the mill out of commission until the damaged sail had been repaired. The six-sailed mill was the most popular of multi-sailed mills. It provided the greatest number of alternative sail combinations, for if one sail became damaged its opposite one could be removed and the mill would work with four sails. Even with three sails removed the sails could be rearranged so alternate sails could be used to maintain the balance. They could, in emergencies, manage, as many four-sailed mills did, with only two sails. It is said that a mill with two sails produces about sixty per cent of the power of that running with four sails. There were seven eight-sailed mills built in England but only Heckington Mill, Lincolnshire, remains with its full complement of sails. Eight sails were generally regarded as the limit to the number that could be usefully employed; after this a mill could become overcrowded with sail.

WINDSHAFTS

The sails were fixed to the windshaft, which was inclined at an angle to the horizontal of between five and fifteen degrees. This enabled some of the weight of the sails to be transferred to the thrust bearing at the tail of the windshaft and so balancing the weight about the neck or front bearing. Also it kept the sails clear of the tapering walls of the tower or the roundhouse of the post mill.

The early windshafts were of oak, tapering from the neck to the tail, with the stocks morticed through it and wedged. An example of this type of early windshaft can be seen at the old mill at Gayton, Merseyside and another example is in The Bridewell Museum, Norwich, which came from the post mill at Thornham, Norfolk. An even more primitive one remains inside the old stone tower mill at Portland Bill, Dorset. These windshafts were weak at the junction of the stocks and being constantly exposed to the weather soon rotted. Later, when cast-iron poll ends were available, the ends were cut off and a poll end bolted and strapped to the old windshaft.

The friction between the windshaft and the neck bearing was a problem. Strips of iron were let into the shaft, while the bearing material itself was, in the early mills, shaped from stone, as at Cat and Fiddle Mill, Derbyshire, or hardwood, but later brass or gunmetal was used. The tail bearing was fitted with an iron 'gudgeon' or 'pintle' which took the thrust, but in earlier mills a separate journal, similar to the neck journal, was provided.

In 1754 John Smeaton introduced cast-iron into millwork and so cast-iron windshafts replaced the timber ones. These windshafts were much smaller, being only about 8 inches diameter compared with up to 24 inches for the timber ones. In the South and East a poll end was cast on the end of the windshaft to carry the sails. This was a double box with openings at right angles, through which the stocks passed and fixed with pinch screws or wedges, although at the six-sailed Ashcombe post mill, Kingston, Sussex, a three-way poll end was used. In Lincolnshire, the North-east, the North-west and occasionally elsewhere a heavy cast-iron 'cross' was hung on the plain end of the windshaft and fixed with iron keys or wedges. The stocks were dispensed with and stouter longer whips, called 'backs', were bolted and strapped to the front of the cross. These cast-iron crosses were very large, spanning about 13 feet and each arm was about 10 inches wide. When a cross was used it enabled the easy removal and refitting of the sails, with the added advantage of being able to fit more than four sails.

Caps

The cap of a tower mill was its most distinguished feature and was considered to be its crowning glory, varying greatly, not only in size but also in shape and construction. Its function was to protect the heavy timbers and machinery housed in the tower.

In most cases the cap frame had two large horizontal beams, called 'sheer trees', which ran on both sides of the cap from the front to the back. At the front, connecting the two sheers, was the 'weather' or 'breast beam' onto which rested the neck bearing of the windshaft. In the centre, securing the top bearing of the upright shaft, was the horizontal 'sprattle beam'. Towards the rear was the 'tail beam', which carried the tail bearing and the thrust block of the windshaft. When a fan was mounted at the rear of the cap the shears were extended to carry it, with the ends of the sheers being connected by a 'cap piece'. If a fan stage was required the sheers were extended even further, with joists between them and boards placed on top to form a platform. Below the cap frame was sometimes built the 'cap circle', which consisted of between five to eight pieces of timber braced to each sheer by 'puncheons' or joists. 'Cap spars' or rafters were erected on top of the cap circle or frame and were sometimes braced by horizontal girts. Caps were generally covered with boarding and often a double layer, the outer layer overlapping the joints of the inner layer and carried down beyond the curb to form a petticoat. To waterproof the cap the boarding was generally covered with painted or tarred canvas; however, many other materials were used including shingles, thatch, copper, lead and even iron plates. A modern method of covering the cap is with aluminium sheeting.

The whole of the cap rests on blocks, rollers or a track rotating on a curb around the top of the tower. The early mills used blocks, made either of wood or gunmetal, with a liberal amount of grease to reduce the friction between the blocks and the curb. This type of curb was called a 'dead curb'. Later a 'live curb' was used, this consisted of iron 'rollers' or wheels, two or three to each side, which ran on either a wooden curb with an iron track on top, or on a cast-iron curb. The final method was the 'shot curb', which consisted of two tracks, one fixed to the curb and the other to the underside of the cap circle, with a number of rollers evenly placed all round the cap. The cap itself was centred by a number of iron 'truckles' or 'truck wheels', fixed to the underside of the cap frame and bearing against the inside of the curb. In the Wirral and Fylde a different method was used to centre the cap. This was the 'well-frame' and comprised four vertical corner posts, hung from the sheers, with a horizontal frame fixed onto the bottom end. The underside of this frame was only a few inches from the dust floor, and had a hole in the centre which fitted around a cast-iron flange ring projecting up through the floor boarding.

Above the windshaft a storm hatch was provided which gave access to the sails, while at the rear a door was generally used to give access to the fan or gallery. Galleries were mostly found in Bedfordshire, Hertfordshire and in East Anglia. Although galleries enabled work to be carried out to the cap with ease, they disturbed the flow of air behind the sails.

Caps varied greatly in shape, there being strong regional designs. Basically five types were constructed—the gabled, the boat-shaped, the wagon-shaped, the domed and the ogee. The gabled caps were the simplest form and found throughout the country. In East Anglia caps resembling an up-turned boat were generally used, while in Kent the wagon-shape were most characteristic. Undoubtedly the finest visual cap was the ogee type, although they had the disadvantage of not fully protecting the front and rear of the cap frame. Round caps were regarded as the best, for these did not disturb the air flow behind the sails as much as the squarer types, like the gabled caps. Some decoration to the cap was indulged in, for many of the round caps were finished with ball or acorn finials, with the petticoat often scalloped.

WINDING THE MILL

It was necessary for the sails of a mill to remain at all times square into the 'eye of the wind', for it was designed and balanced to resist pressure from the front and not from the rear. Much damage occurred to a mill that was 'tail-winded' by a sudden change in the direction of the wind—the cloths or shutters could be blown out of the sails and even the mill itself could be blown over, in the case of a post mill, or the cap blown off, in the case of a tower mill. It was, therefore, necessary to be able to turn the mill into the wind, and this was known as luffing or 'winding the mill'.

The simplest form of winding gear was the 'tail pole,' which was worked manually and generally used on post mills, but sometimes on the earlier, smaller smock and tower mills. In the post mill the tail pole passed down from the body of the mill and through the main steps or ladder at the rear. When the mill was at work these steps generally rested on the ground, adding some support against the pressure of the wind on the face of the mill. Before luffing, the steps had to be raised by means of a lever, called a 'talthur', pivoted on the tail pole. This lever, that had one end attached to the bottom tread of the steps by a chain, could be held down by an iron pin, keeping the steps, which was hinged at the top, up and so enabling the miller to push against the tail pole with his back, or with his shoulders against a 'yoke' attached to the tail pole. Later a small winch was fixed to the end of the tail pole, a chain or rope was fastened to this and hooked to one of a number of chain posts set in a circle around the mill. The winch was turned by a hand-wheel thus moving the mill to a new position. This device can still be seen at the Cat and Fiddle Mill, Dale Abbey, Derbyshire. The tail pole was supported by a link rod or chain from the top of the mill body, taking the weight of the steps when they were raised. On occasions a cart wheel was attached to the end of the tail pole, which rested on the ground supporting its weight. The early smock and tower mills were also winded by means of a tail pole, suspended from the cap and reaching almost to the ground, strengthened with additional braces at each side. Examples can be seen at the restored mills at West Wratting, Cambridgeshire and Herringfleet, Suffolk.

As smock and tower mills increased in height it was necessary to improve the method of turning the cap. The first advance consisted of a rack, fixed to the outside of the curb, and geared through a timber worm. This worm was at first cut out of a large single piece of hardwood, but later it was made from cast-iron and attached at the rear of the cap. It was driven through gearing by a chain wheel, set at right angles to the tower, over which an endless chain passed to the ground and onto which the miller pulled, moving the cap as required. In some cases the worm was replaced by a spur gear and the rack was mounted either on the top or on the outside of the curb, with the chain wheel set parallel to the mill. These racks were at first made of wood, but later formed in cast-iron. The construction of the chain wheel varied, being made either of wood, or wood with iron 'Y' forks, or all iron with 'Y' forks. These wheels were commonly called 'Y' wheels.

A fully automatic method of luffing was introduced in 1745 when Edmund Lee patented the 'fantail'. This was a small wind wheel comprising generally six or eight vanes, but occasionally five, seven or ten were used. These vanes, formed of matchboarding strengthened at the edges with battens, were each bolted to wooden spokes or 'fan stocks' which were fitted into the sockets of the metal 'star wheel'. This was mounted on an iron shaft fitted to the 'fan spars'. Each vane was connected at its tip to the adjacent vane by an iron rod, and in addition iron rings were fixed to both sides of the fan stocks to strengthen the fantail.

The fantail was set at right angles to the sails, mounted, in the case of a tower or smock mill, at the rear of the cap. It was connected through reduction gearing to a rack on top of the curb, or to a worm or a spur pinion as used in the wheel and chain method. While the sails remained square into the wind the fantail remained stationary, being sheltered by the mill, but as soon as the wind changed direction it struck the side of the vanes setting it in motion, turning the mill until the sails again faced into the wind. A wheel and chain was sometimes used in conjunction with the fantail and when the fantail became damaged it was disconnected so the mill could be luffed manually.

The fantail was also applied to the post mill and various methods were used, but the Sussex and East Anglian types were generally adopted. With the Sussex type the fantail was mounted on the tail pole, being carried on an upright timber-framed carriage running on a pair of iron wheels on a track around the mill. The drive was taken down to the bottom of the carriage, where it divided to drive each wheel, which ran on either a tramway formed of elm or oak slabs, or a gravel track. This method was generally used in Sussex, but was occasionally found elsewhere and can still be seen at the mills at Argos Hill and Cross-in-Hand, Sussex. This method imposed a great strain on the tail pole itself, as well as being positioned so far back from the body of the mill that it acted as a weather vane, swinging the mill from side to side.

In East Anglia, and particularly Suffolk, the tail pole was either removed completely or cut off at the point where it projected beyond the steps. The carriage wheels were fitted to the end of the steps and the drive taken to the wheels. This method of mounting the fantail was structurally sounder than the Sussex type, but the Sussex type, being further back, caught the wind easier thus turning the mill closer to the 'eye of the wind'.

Another variation was to fit the fantail on the roof of the mill; the remains of this type can be seen at Ramsey, Essex, with the drive taken vertically downwards and then at right angles to a worm wheel fixed on the main post below the body of the mill. The fourth method was to fix the fantail on the roof and take the drive down the steps to the wheel at the bottom, as at Icklesham, Sussex. The final variation was to take the drive from the roof to a rack on top of the roundhouse.

BRAKE WHEELS AND GEARING
Fixed to the windshaft was the 'brake wheel', so called from the fact that the band brake, which stops the mill, is fitted around its rim. The earliest type of brake wheel was the 'compass arm' wheel, where two, or occasionally three arms were morticed and wedged through the windshaft to form a cross. To the ends of these arms were fitted four, six or eight 'cants' on which curved timbers were fixed to form a rim. This form of wheel had a serious disadvantage, for the mortices weakened the windshaft at the point where most strength was needed. In the early part of the eighteenth century the 'clasp arm' or 'griped arm' wheel was introduced. With this type of wheel the four arms were halved together forming a square through which the windshaft passed. Oak was generally used for these wheels, with the arms, cants and rims often doubled to increase the strength. The wheel was hung on the windshaft and wedged, usually four to each corner. The circular iron windshaft usually had a square formed on it to carry the brake wheel. In the latter half of the eighteenth century cast-iron brake wheels were introduced. Some were

composite wheels with timber rims fixed to cast iron 'spiders', while others were constructed entirely of iron with the geared rims either bolted on separately, as at Buttrum's Mill, Woodbridge, Suffolk, or more often cast as one unit.

The early teeth on these brake wheels were simply wooden pegs morticed through the rim and pinned at the rear. These teeth engaged with a lantern pinion-type gear. Later wheels had proper cogs fitted, not only to wooden wheels but also to iron ones, these being known as morticed wheels. These cogs were roughly shaped, fitted to the wheel and finally finished in position with the shanks fitted, where possible, through the rim of the wheel. The cogs were secured with wooden or iron pins driven obliquely through the shank, or with dovetailed wedges driven between two shanks, or sometimes having the shanks split and wedges driven in. Apple and hornbeam were regarded as two of the best woods to use for cogs, but any hardwood was suitable provided it could be easily worked. These teeth, if well lubricated with grease or linseed oil, would last half a lifetime. Some post mills had two rows of cogs, one to drive the machinery and the other the stones, while Madingley Mill, Cambridgeshire, had cogs that were staggered, probably to avoid backlash. To prevent uneven wear on the cogs a 'hunting cog' was introduced, thus avoiding simple gear ratio and ensuring that the two wheels would mesh together differently at each revolution. Iron teeth were often used: these were cast in segments, and occasionally replaced the wooden cogs on the clasp arm wheels which had previously been cut off flush.

The most common form of 'brake' was a massive wooden contracting band acting on the brake wheel. This was usually of elm, in six or eight sections, joined together with iron plates and bolts. It extended almost all round the brake wheel, being fastened at one end, while the other end was attached to a horizontal beam, called the 'brake lever'. This lever was extremely heavy, capable by its own weight of holding the brake on the brake wheel. The brake was released by raising the lever by means of a rope attached to the end, which passed over a sheave in the roof above and down to a floor below. The lever was raised until an iron pin, fixed in the lever, engaged with a swinging hook above, holding the lever in an 'off' position. To apply the brake again it was only necessary to pull on the rope raising the lever so disengaging the hook. Occasionally iron was used both for the lever and the brake band, which sometimes was fixed with wooden blocks. At Rolvenden and Wittersham Mills, Kent, the brakes are unusual, being formed of a combination of wood and iron—wood below and iron above the centre line. At Patcham Mill, Sussex, there is no brake lever and the brake is applied by an iron chain wheel, situated outside the cap, which through a number of bevels is connected to a screw-driving bevel connected to the brake.

In the early post mill only a single pair of stones was used, receiving its drive direct from the brake wheel. As the post mill increased in size and power an additional pair of stones was installed in the tail, driven by a tail wheel fitted near the end of the windshaft. Like the early post mill, the early tower mill also contained only one pair of stones, being driven by a central vertical spindle. The revolving cap made it impossible to increase the capacity of the mill in the same way as with the post mill, but the problem was solved by the introduction of the 'upright shaft' and spur gearing. The upright shaft was driven by the 'wallower', which received its drive direct from the brake wheel. In the post mill the brake wheel was situated not too far behind the neck bearing, while in the tower mill it was further back, for this had to mesh with the wallower which was located centrally in the tower. The wallower was driven by and situated behind the brake wheel. The early wallowers were face gears of the lantern pinion-type, comprising two solid hardwood discs between which were fitted a ring of wooden staves. These staves were secured either with pins, or with wedges driven into the split end and so opening it out. The lantern pinion was superseded by the 'trundle' or 'cow-pop' gear. This gear was similar to the lantern pinion, but with the top disc removed and an increased number of shorter staves. Later bevel gears were introduced, first of the compass or clasp arm construction, but finally of iron with all the variations previously described for brake wheels.

The upright shaft in the post mill was originally of wood, but later of iron, and was generally situated in the breast, although sometimes they were fitted in the tail in addition. Both wood and iron shafts were used in tower mills, while sometimes sections of both materials were installed, called 'graft shafts'. For easier installation the shaft in the tower mills were mainly fitted in two or more sections, jointed with a dog-clutch type of coupling. Wooden upright shafts were up to 18 inches square, being square, octagonal, sixteen-sided, or round in shape. Iron shafts were about one third the size of wooden ones and were generally square or round. The top bearing on the shaft was a plain, journal bearing fitted, in the case of a post mill, on a horizontal spindle beam framed between the two top side girts, while in the tower mill it was fitted on the side of the horizontal sprattle beam of the cap frame. To prevent whip in the length of the shaft an intermediate bearing was introduced and at the bottom a combined thrust and journal bearing was used. This was originally a brass pot bearing let into a beam, with folding wedges to adjust the level of the beam, so lining up the bottom bearing with the top bearing. Later, the cast-iron bridging box, with four adjustable screws, replaced the former bearing.

Mounted on the upright shaft was the 'great spur wheel' to which was geared the stone nuts, driving the stones either from above, called 'over-drift', or from below, called 'underdrift'. The first great spur wheels were of compass-arm construction with the arms morticed through the upright shaft, but these were superseded by clasp arm wheels, composite iron and wooden wheels, and wheels constructed entirely of iron. Originally the great spur wheel drove the stone through small pinions of the lantern type, but later these were replaced by solid, wooden stone nuts morticed for hardwood cogs, which had the appearance of a wooden cart hub. After these, iron stone nuts with wooden cogs morticed in and finally ones made completely of iron were all used.

It was essential that the stone nut could be thrown out of gear, thus disengaging any pair of stones when not required for use. When the stones were overdrift each stone nut was mounted on a 'quant', the top bearing of which was housed in a 'glut box' which enabled half the bearing to be moved to one side so the stone nut could be moved clear of the great spur wheel. With underdrift stones the wooden stone nuts were disengaged by removal of 'slip-cogs', these being cogs easily removed by extracting their fixing pins. When iron pinions were employed these were frequently mounted on a square on the stone spindle, being lifted out of gear by means of a screw, a rack and pinion, or a rigger.

MILLSTONES
Millstones were arranged in pairs; only the upper runner stone revolved—the lower bed stone was stationary. They varied in size from 3 feet 6 inches to 5 feet in diameter, but about 4 feet was accepted as the most satisfactory. A stone of this size, weighing over a ton, was geared to run at a speed of about 125 revolutions per minute.

Stones were required to be of a high quality and were both expensive to buy and difficult to find. The finest stone quarried in Britain was the peak stone, a millstone grit, from the Peak District of Derbyshire, but many inferior local stones were used including sandstones from the West Midlands and granite from Wales and Dartmoor. The peak stones were used for animal feed. Another stone was the blue or cullin, originally used for general purposes, quarried at Neider Mending and imported from Cologne. The finest of all stones were French burrs quarried at La Ferté-Sous-Jouarre in the Paris Basin. The material, found only in small quantities, was cut, shaped and pieced together to form a stone. These pieces were jointed in cement and had iron hoops shrunk on round them to hold the pieces together and backed with plaster of Paris. Sometimes an iron ring was let into the plaster round the eye of the runner stone with the maker's name. French stone were generally used for grinding flour and required dressing about every twelve days.

The stones were divided into three areas: the first, about one third of the radius from the rim, was called the skirt, the second the breast and the third, near the centre, the eye. The surface of the stones had to be prepared with great care and it was necessary to produce a perfectly smooth surface. A wooden 'paint staff', about 4 feet long, 3 inches wide and 5 inches deep, was used with 'tiver', a composition of red iron oxide mixed with water, applied to the staff. The staff was drawn over the stone to detect the high spots and these were gently rubbed down with burr stone until perfect. Each time the stone dresser dressed a pair of stones the staff was tested against a 'proof staff', which was usually a long, narrow, cast-iron plate mounted in a case.

The bed stone was dressed level, but the runner stone was slightly hollowed towards the eye so that the grain was forced out towards the periphery enabling the grain to be ground and not suddenly flattened, clogging the stone. This hollow was called the 'swallow' and for the depth the stone dresser used a gauge or 'eye staff'. The stone was marked out into eight or ten equal harps and these were sub-divided into alternate lands and furrows. The furrows were cut to a depth which varied between $\frac{1}{4}$ and $\frac{3}{4}$ of an inch and finished with a sharp arris on one side and an even slope up to the land on the other. A series of fine parallel grooves, called 'stitching', were cut into the surface of each land, up to sixteen cracks per inch. These were of uniform depth at the skirt, becoming lighter until they died out in about the middle of the breast. The dressing was so arranged that when the stones were in their working position the furrows crossed at each revolution, cutting the grain with the action of scissor blades. The stones would soon wear, ceasing to grind efficiently and they had to be redressed. To do this the runner stone was raised by a lever or crowbar until it was possible to insert a big triangular wedge, called a 'scotch wedge', beneath. A rope was then passed through the eye and the stone finally raised, either by means of a pulley or by a sling over the windshaft, onto its edge. Sometimes the stone was raised by means of a worm-and-chain tackle, with a pair of Lewis bolts or 'clams' inserted into holes in the edge of the stone. The runner stone was laid to one side for dressing, while the bed stone was dressed in position.

The stones were dressed with 'mill bills', made from best quality high carbon steel, resembling a double-edged wedge. When new these mill bills were about 11 inches long by $1\frac{1}{2}$ inches square in the centre and weighed about $3\frac{1}{2}$ pounds. With constant grinding and forging this was gradually reduced until, when something less than 2 pounds, they were regarded as being too light and discarded. The mill bills were held in a wooden handle or 'thrift', generally made from ash but sometimes from chestnut or beech. When grinding cattle-feed a pointed mill bill, called a 'pick', was used.

In the nineteenth century stone dressing was a trade of its own, and many pairs of stone dressers travelled around the country from mill to mill. Often the back of the left hand of these men became discoloured by small particles of steel that embedded themselves under the skin. Before the stone dresser was engaged the miller would ask him to 'show his steel'. Later, when the milling industry was on the decline, the dressing of the stone was generally undertaken by the miller himself.

The bed stone was supported on a timber frame, sometimes on a 'hurst frame' standing on the floor, but generally set in the floor itself and wedged up off the frame until it lay in a horizontal plane. Above the bed stone was the runner stone, carried on a cast-iron 'stone spindle' which passed through the bed stone, with a 'bridging box' and thrust bearing at its lower end resting on the 'bridge tree'. Around the neck of the spindle was the 'neck box', consisting of a cast-iron box with three brass pads and one wooden pad with a stem which hung down called a 'grease wedge', and this could be removed to enable the bearing to be greased. The whole bearing was let into the bed stone and wedged. On top and screwed to this box bearing was a 'hackle plate' which held a leather washer to prevent dust entering the bearing. The runner stone was supported on the top or 'cock head' of the stone spindle by either a 'bridge', a bow-shaped iron bar, or a 'gimbal', a stout iron ring. The bridge or gimbal was let into the runner stone, across the eye, and caulked. They both received their drive from a cast-iron 'mace' located on a tapered square on the stone spindle. In the case of the bridge, the mace had a recess on the top in which the bridge sat, while when a gimbal was used the mace was provided with trunnions on which rested the two recesses formed in the underside of the gimbal. In early mills an iron cross or 'rynd' was used instead of the mace and bridge or gimbal bar; this had four arms let into the runner stone. The disadvantage of the rynd was that it was rigid and therefore the runner stone was difficult to balance.

When the stones were underdrift the mace or bridge had provision made for the 'damsel', a three or four-sided spindle used to shake the shoe. When overdrift stones were used the mace had two slots provided on each side into which the quant engaged.

It was, of course, essential that the stone spindle was vertical so that the runner stone ran true, and careful adjustment was required to allow the stone to rotate in a horizontal plane. To test this a wooden bar, called the 'jack staff', was fitted over the stone spindle. This had an upright quill wedged into a hole near the outer end and could be adjusted by means of a thumb-nail screw which opened and closed a slit. The stone spindle was gently rotated from below as the miller watched the quill for any deviation. If not true the stone spindle was corrected by adjusting the four pinching screws in the bridging box.

The runner stone had to be balanced and this was achieved by running lead into pockets cut into the top of the stone. Later, Clark and Dunham's patent balances were occasionally fitted. These were cylindrical metal pockets set into the stone on opposite sides near the rim and contained a number of lead discs on a metal screw. The position of the discs could be raised or lowered on the screw and so balance the stone.

The grain, stored on the bin floor above the stone floor, was fed by gravity through a grain spout to the square wooden 'hoppers'. The hoppers were supported on a wooden frame, known as the 'horse', which rested on top of the removable timber casing around the stones, called the 'vat' or 'tun'. From the hopper the grain entered an inclined tapered trough called the 'shoe'. The shoe pivoted freely from the horse, at one end, and was held at the other end against the damsel, in the case of underdrift stones, or against a square on the quant, in the case of overdrift stones. As the damsel or quant revolved, it shook the shoe causing the grain to fall down the shoe and into the eye of the stone. As the speed of the stones increased the more the shoe was shaken and so the faster the grain fell. The flow of grain could be regulated by means of a 'crook string'. This was a cord attached at one end to the lower end of the shoe and at the other end to a 'twist peg' on the meal floor below. The miller could by operating the cord vary the angle of the shoe and so the amount of grain entering the stones. There was sometimes in addition a small adjustable 'gate' in the shoe, operated by another cord, that assisted in controlling the flow of grain. The shoe was tensioned against the revolving damsel or quant by a simple wooden spring, the 'miller's willow', which was a short length of willow, attached to the top of the vat, with a cord from its end to the shoe.

The grain fell from the shoe, through the eye of the runner stone, and was ground between the lands of the runner and bed stone. The meal was forced along the furrows to the outer edge of the stones, finally being caught between the stones and the vat. The meal had to be collected in one place. So small metal 'paddles' were fixed to the rim of the runner stone, and as it rotated they swept the space between the vat and stones pushing the meal through the meal hole into the meal spout and to the bin below. Sometimes the meal was fed directly into sacks, a wooden coathanger-shaped bar with a metal spike at each end was used to hold the sack open.

The stones had to have a constant supply of grain, for if the stones ran short of grain they might touch, causing the stones to become blunt, and so alarm bells were fitted to give warning when the hoppers were becoming empty. The usual type of alarm consisted of a piece of leather placed inside the hopper, near the bottom, and attached to it was a length of cord that passed out through the opposite side of the hopper and was connected to a bell. The grain in the hopper held down the leather, keeping the cord taut. As the grain ran out the weight on the leather was removed, and the leather rose, making the bell fall against one of the moving parts.

To produce meal of the correct texture three points had to be considered: the amount of grain fed to the stones, the speed of the stones and the gap between the stones. This gap was adjusted by raising and lowering the runner stone, a process called 'tentering'. This operation was carried out by adjusting the end of the 'bridge tree', which carried the footstep bearing of the stone spindle. The bridge tree was pivoted at one end and supported at the other end by the 'bray' or 'brayer', while the free end of the bray was supported by the 'steelyard'—a long iron lever which passed over a fulcrum and had considerable leverage. The distance between the stones necessitated adjustment of a few hundredths of an inch and a 'lighter screw' was provided that passed either through the bray at its junction with the steelyard or, when this was dispensed with, through the bridge tree itself. The bridge tree, and consequently the runner stone, could be raised and lowered by means of this screw and so the gap adjusted between the stones. Once set this gap was kept constant. As speed increased, however, the runner stone tended to rise, and to counteract this centrifugal governors were installed.

These governors consisted of two metal bob weights, which were generally driven by a belt either from the upright shaft or from the stone spindle. The bob weights hung down when the mill was at rest, but as it turned, the weights flew out raising the sliding collar on the shaft. As the speed increased or decreased the weights moved in and out and the collar thus moved up and down. Attached to the collar was the steelyard, so as the collar moved the steelyard followed. This rise and fall was transmitted through the bray, bridge tree and stone spindle to the runner stone and maintained a constant gap between the two stones. At Bembridge tower mill a primitive arrangement may be seen. At the lower end of the upright shaft there is a pulley belt going off to the pulley on the shaft of a governor. When the weights rise they pull on two cords which pass between floor and ceiling twice before lifting the end of the bridge tree.

SACK HOISTS

It was necessary to raise the grain to the floor above the stone floor so that it could feed down to the stones and for this a sack hoist was used.

When first used it consisted simply of a rope and pulley fixed to a timber beam projecting from the gable of the mill. Later an endless hand rope, passing over a large wooden pulley onto which a long drum of smaller diameter was attached, was used. When the rope was pulled the sack chain was wound up on the drum.

The mechanically driven hoist comprised a long horizontal wooden drum attached to the sack 'bollard'—a wooden shaft with wooden battens nailed along its length. The sack chain was fixed to the bollard, passing down through the hinged double trapdoors in the floors to the ground floor. In the post mill, the drive to the sack hoist was generally taken from a wooden pulley mounted on the windshaft close to the brake wheel and in the case of tower or smock mills from the upright shaft by gearing and a countershaft. A slack belt or chain was passed round the drive pulley or shaft and up round the drum attached to the end of the sack bollard. Generally a timber solepiece, operated by a lever with a cord attached, was used to tighten the belt. When the sack cord was pulled, which like the sack chain passed to the ground floor, it raised the solepiece, together with the drum and bollard and tightened the belt. The tightened belt would drive the drum and thus wind the chain, raising the sack as long as the cord was held. When the sack reached the bin floor the cord was slackened off, the solepiece dropped, and the belt no longer drove.

Another method used for the drive was a friction wheel, acting generally on the outer rim of the tail wheel in the case of a post mill, and on the lower surface of the wallower in the case of a tower or smock mill. A wooden pulley was attached to the end of the sack bollard, to which was fixed a lever pivoted at one end with a cord at the other. As the cord was pulled this raised the lever and the pulley engaged with the wallower or tail wheel.

Bolters and Wire Machines

When the meal left the stones it had to be dressed so that the bran and middlings could be removed. In the medieval mill this work was not executed by the miller but by a meal or bolter man, or by the baker and was sifted by hand in a sieve or 'temse'. Later a 'bolter' was installed and the work carried out in the mill itself. The bolter consisted of a cylindrical wooden casing into which was fitted a wooden frame on a rotating inclined axis. This frame was covered with a seamless, woollen bolting cloth, reinforced with leather straps, and fastened at each end with a drawstring. The lower end of the frame was open and the other end had a coarse mesh net. The flour entered the top end of the bolter by an overhead hopper, passing through the mesh net to remove any foreign matter. As the frame revolved the meal passed through causing the cloth to sag until it brushed against a number of longitudinal wooden bars which vibrated and shook the flour through the cloth. The bran and middling passed out at the lower end. Early bolters were worked by hand, but later power was taken from the main shaft, generally by a pulley and belt but sometimes by gearing.

The 'wire machine' replaced the bolter. The principle was similar, but was different in design, being a fixed wooden cylinder covered in sections by wire gauze of various degrees of fineness. A spindle, with a series of longitudinal brushes attached, passed down the centre of the cylinder and as it rotated the meal was brushed through the gauze with the bran tailing out at the end. The meal was fed to the bolter and wire machine by a shoe, similar to the stones and, like the stones, the flow was generally regulated by cords and feed pegs, with the shoe being knocked by a double cam on the spindle. Occasionally small governors were used to control the feed.

Another form and older type of flour dresser was the 'jog-scry', this consisted of a number of inclined rectangular sieves with several grades of mesh, each overlapping the one below, and was jerked up and down in order to move the meal, which was fed in at the top, down each sieve. Other machines that were used were 'smutters', which removed the black fungus which attacks wheat, 'separators' and 'screeners', which removed the dust and grit before grinding, modern 'oat crushers', 'bean kibblers' and 'centrifugal flour dressers'. In the North-west of England 'groat machines' were used for preparing oats for porridge. The oats were first roasted in a kiln, next to the mill, after which they passed through a pair of stones to split the husks off the grain, and then through the groat machine to remove the husks by a fan.

All these machines were driven by a variety of methods. In a tower or smock mill the drive was generally taken from a bevel drive, either from a separate wheel or a bevel ring on the great spur wheel. With the post mill the most common method was to take the drive from the brake or tail wheel by a skew-geared pinion. In both the tower and post mills the finial drive was usually by a belt.

PART TWO

Preserved Windmills and Their History

Bedfordshire
STEVINGTON MILL   NGR SP992528

Stevington post mill is the finest and most complete windmill in Bedfordshire, although no longer capable of working. Situated in an open field
her appearance is much as in 1929 when Thurston Hopkins wrote:

'. . . I could hardly believe my eyes. The cloth was furled neatly on all four
sweeps as they arose over a little hump across the green fields; the mill was in
perfect condition and freshly painted . . . the roof, of red corrugated iron, is
not curved or pointed but is four sided. . . .'

The mill was probably built in 1770, for on Thomas Jefferys' map of
1765 no mill is shown, but the date 1770 is inscribed on one of the crosstrees. The mill was almost certainly built for Richard Pool, a baker, but
it seems probable that he did not operate the mill himself for in 1803 the
miller was James Paselow. On the death of Richard Pool, in 1804, the
mill passed to his son, William, who was obliged to mortgage the mill and
by 1837 she had passed to the Green family—his creditors. At about this
time the mill was let to Robert Franklin and then, on his death, to his
widow, Ann. In 1849 Edmund Favell of Stevington purchased the mill
from Thomas Abbott Green for £470. Mr Favell sold the mill in 1868 to
William Raban, a relative of Favell, who was followed by James Raban
who worked her until 1917 when Alfred Raban, the grandson, sold her to
George Field.

By 1921, although the mill was still in working order, she had become
very dilapidated and in September of that year work began on the
rebuilding. The work was carried out by Mr P. W. G. Keech, a carpenter
and wheelwright of Stevington, with the assistance of five or six men.
The complete body of the mill was lifted off the main post while the pintle
was repaired and the crosstrees, which had become out of level over the
years, were raised. The body of the mill was reboarded and the framing
repaired. The stones were removed and replaced by stones from Milton
Ernest Mill, this work being undertaken by Messrs Course of Bedford.
They also removed the old tentering gear and installed the present one.
The work was completed in some twelve weeks, silencing the many local
critics who thought the task impossible, but it was a further six weeks
before there was sufficient wind to work her. Inside the mill is an inscription on one of the crosstrees 'Rebuilt 1921 P. Keech'. After the rebuilding Mr Field continued to work the mill commercially until about 1936.

The mill was acquired, in 1951, by the County Council from the repre-
sentatives of George Field and the mill was repaired, under the supervision of the County Architect, by Messrs Clayson & Son of Harrold to

mark the occasion of the Festival of Britain. The mill was probably the last windmill in the country to work with four common sails. The sails were replaced in 1958 by Messrs E. Hole & Son of Burgess Hill, Sussex and further repairs were carried out on these in 1972.

BRILL MILL NGR SP652142

Brill Mill stands at the top of a steep declivity overlooking the Vale of Oxford towards the Cotswolds. There was at one time three mills standing on the common. The surviving mill was erected in or about 1680 and not 1668 as had previously been thought. She was evidently rebuilt in 1757, using the old windshaft and main post, for in the account book kept by William Snell for that year the following appears:

> Nov. 2. Expenses of Rebuilding a Windmill which was blown down at Brill, exclusive of value of old materials and which Mill is now lett to John Atkins at per Ann £9. £175.5.0.

Also recorded in the same book is that in 1805 the mill was occupied by William Adkins, who was also known to have been miller in 1796.

In 1847 William Wellford was miller, followed by John Wellford and by the 1860s Francis Hayes was operating the mill. Henry Nixey took over the mill in 1865 and it was at this time that the original roundhouse was constructed. The mill remained in the Nixey family for the remainder of her working life, Henry being succeeded by Andrew, who was also a corn dealer and brickmaker, and finally, at the turn of the century, by Albert. The mill was in regular use until 1916, though she operated on occasions until the mid 1920s, when Mr Nixey retired to take over a smallholding.

The mill was bought and preserved, in 1929, by Major H. L. Aubrey Fletcher, being handed over to trustees who maintained her until the war. During the war she was damaged by soldiery after which she was presented to Buckinghamshire County Council. She was severely damaged in storms in the spring of 1947 when one of the sails broke, leaving the remaining three swinging in the wind and causing the windshaft to break free, distorting the body of the mill. Early in 1948 Stanley Freese inspected the mill and arranged with Frank Boothman of the County Council Planning Department to carry out repairs. The roundhouse was rebuilt by Arthur White, whose father built the original one; four new sails were fitted and the mill generally repaired, restoring her to something like her original appearance. In 1966 an estimate of £3,000 for the mill's restoration was said to be prohibitive, and repair work was delayed with the mill being fenced off. Work was finally commenced in August 1967, when the main post was found to be out of true. The County Council then reinforced the mill with iron stanchions at each corner. During gales, in September 1973, one of the sail stocks broke at the poll end causing some damage as it fell. With the help of the Historic Works and Building Group of the Chiltern Society the remaining sails were removed, being replaced in 1975.

45

Buckinghamshire
LACEY GREEN MILL   NGR SP819009

For a long time the condition of this old smock mill, which stands on a windy summit of the Chilterns at Lacey Green, was considered to be 'too far gone' to be restored. The possibility of saving the mill was first considered at the inaugural meeting of the Historic Works and Building Group of the Chiltern Society in 1967, but it was not until 1971 that the Society reached agreement with the owners on her preservation and secured a twenty-five-year lease on the mill. Before work was commenced David Wray prepared a detailed perspective drawing, showing the mill and her machinery as she must have been when originally working, and this drawing formed the basis of the restoration. The aim of the Society was to restore the mill to her original working order, with the assistance of a team of volunteers, at an estimated cost of £3,500. Christopher Wallis M.I.C.E. was appointed engineer in charge of the undertaking. The decayed mill was at this time 2 feet out of plumb and first the cap, cap frame and windshaft were removed, by means of a crane, in order to remove the weight from the body of the mill. After this the twisted and leaning body was straightened and the body was strengthened and held permanently upright by a skin of plywood sheathing concealed between the inner and outer boarding. This was followed by the fitting of the cap and windshaft, the replacing and the renewal of the floors and machinery and finally the fitting of the sails and fantail. Most of the plant for the restoration work was loaned by various firms free of charge, while much money was donated by numerous people and in 1973 the Department of the Environment agreed to give a grant of £1,720 to the Society.

The mill is the oldest surviving smock mill in the country. She was reported to have been built in 1650 and certainly much of the machinery—the brake wheel, windshaft, wallower and mainshaft—is typical of mid-seventeenth century construction. She was originally built at Chesham and moved, in 1821, to her present site on the orders of the Duke of Buckingham. The mill was dismantled piece by piece, incised with Roman numerals, curious cross strokes and squares, and re-assembled on her new site. At this time a fantail was added, together with a pair of patent sails. The last miller appears to have been John Cheshire, whose family also ran the mill at nearby Loosley Green. She ceased work in about 1914–15 after which she was used as a weekend cottage. By the 1930s the mill had become dilapidated; an appeal was launched, with some repair work being undertaken in 1934 in order to prevent her from collapse. Two years later an attempt to preserve the mill failed. During

46

the Second World War the mill served as a 'look out' post for the local
Home Guard after which she was used as a farm store. Finally she be-
came so derelict that she was thought to be past saving until the Chiltern
Society undertook the repair work.

PITSTONE MILL   NGR SP945156

The exact date of the construction of Pitstone Mill is not certain, but carved on a side girt is the date 1627 which makes this the oldest-dated mill in the country. It is known from documentary evidence that at this time work was being carried out on a mill at Pitstone when payments were made to carpenters and a new gable was fitted. Also in the mill is a second date, 1749, which probably refers to the rebuilding of the mill in which some old timbers were incorporated.

In 1840 the mill, together with a nearby watermill, was owned by the Grand Junction Canal Company and worked by Benjamin Anstee. Two years later both mills were purchased by Francis Beesley who worked them both himself. He continued to work the windmill until 1874 when he sold her to Lord Brownlow, who owned the Ashridge Estate, for £400. The mill was then let to the Hawkins' family who had for many years rented the Pitstone Green Farm. In 1895 much repair work was undertaken, but seven years later a freak storm tail-winded the mill causing considerable damage. The sails were blown forward, causing the tail bearing of the windshaft to fly through the roof. The sails then revolved the wrong way, crashing into the wall of the roundhouse. The mill never again worked commercially and soon became derelict.

The Ashridge Estate was broken up and sold in the 1920s and the mill became the property of the Hawkins' family in 1924. By 1937 the mill was in a state of collapse and the owner, Leonard Hawkins, offered the mill to the National Trust. Immediately the National Trust engaged Bushell Brothers of Tring to repair and strengthen the structure and a pair of small mock sails were added. However, much of the character of the mill was lost.

It was some twenty years before any more work was undertaken on the mill. By this time she had once again deteriorated and it was found that one of the quarterbars was sinking into the decayed crosstree. At this time the late Stanley Freese noticed that the date carved on a beam was not 1697 but, in fact, 1627. As the mill was in danger of collapse temporary repairs were carried out. Vertical posts were inserted to support the body of the mill and four extra quarterbars were fitted to the main post, tied to the existing quarterbars.

The Pitstone Windmill Committee was formed in 1963 in an effort to restore the mill. An appeal for funds was launched and approximately £1,000 was collected. All labour on the restoration was voluntary and every effort made to return the mill to her original

appearance. The sails were made at Aylesbury College of Further Education while, as only the heaviest machinery remained in the mill, other machinery was obtained from derelict mills. In 1970 the work on the mill was successfully submitted for a 'Countryside in 1970' award.

BOURN MILL   NGR TL312580

The small post mill at Bourn, which stands almost on the parish boundary with Caxton, is generally regarded as the oldest surviving windmill in
the country, although the mill at Pitstone, Buckinghamshire, is the earliest dated mill. The earliest reference to the mill at Bourn is 1636, discovered by the late General H. Hendly following research into the mill's
history and the discovery of an old deed of 1653. In this deed there is reference to the date 1636, when Thomas Cook purchased the mill from
John Cook, thus proving that the mill was in existence before this date.
Bourn Mill herself is extremely small—the body being only 10 feet 3
inches by 14 feet 6 inches and the overall height 31 feet 6 inches—and
although much altered and extended the body is original retaining her
simple, medieval, pitched roof, but the machinery within the mill has
been renewed, some of it twice.

The deed of 1653 throws a little light on the mill's early history for this
deed was a conveyance of the 'Wind Mill together with a little Corne
Garane' from Thomas Cook to William Smythe, a blacksmith from the
neighbouring village of Caxton. Inside the mill is an inscription 'E.
Bismur 1758' on a stud to the first floor, but who he was is now unknown. Little more is known of the mill's early history until 1779 when
John Butler, a local farmer, took a lease on the mill before finally purchasing her in 1799. In 1832 he died leaving the mill, mill house and land
to his niece, Mary Heywood, and her husband, Eliezer, of Huntingdon.
They sold the property, in 1836, to Joshua Hipwell of Toft for £550, who
continued to work the mill until his death in 1866, when she passed to his
son, William. He remained there for only a few years, giving up the mill
which had, by this time, been acquired by the Belham family. The mill
was repaired in 1874 and it was probably at this time that the Papworths
became associated with the mill—first Zaccheus until the 1880s, then
William and finally, in about 1910, by George. The mill continued to be
worked solely by wind until about 1924 when an oil engine was introduced to assist the grinding.

The mill finally ceased work in 1927 and in 1931 was purchased by Sir
Alfred Bossom and Mr Mansfield Forbes for £45. These two gentlemen
and Mr Pentelow, the previous owner, contributed towards the repairs of
the mill, while George Papworth, the last miller, gave his services free.
The repairs were undertaken by Hunt Brothers, the millwrights of
Soham. On 3rd June 1932, the mill was officially transferred from Mr
Pentelow to the Cambridge Preservation Society, when a celebration
took place. This included singers and fiddlers, dressed in Elizabethan
clothes, and a 'Don Quixote' on horseback who tilted at the mill. Mr Pap-

worth continued to live at the mill house after the mill had been handed over and continued to be caretaker. The mill has since been kept in excellent repair by the Society and steel angles have been introduced to strengthen the body. The mill was extensively repaired in 1965.

GREAT CHISHILL MILL   NGR TL413388

Close to the county border with Essex stands a fine post mill and the only one with a fantail to survive within the county. The present mill bears an inscription 'W.A.1726', but was rebuilt in 1819 from material from an old thatched post mill on the same site for Henry Andrews by Chuck of Barley. The mill remained in the Andrews family for almost one hundred years; Henry was followed by James, who in turn was followed in 1850 by the latter's son, Henry, who remained miller for over thirty years before being succeeded by Job and finally, at the end of the nineteenth century, by Alfred. During this period much work was carried out on the mill: in 1877 a new post was put in by a Cambridge millwright, in 1890 four patent sails and a fantail were added, while at some time the platform at the top of the ladder was enclosed and a lean-to porch added.

Alfred Andrews was followed by John Pegram, the mill remaining in his family for the remainder of her working life. John Pegram was followed by Joseph who, in July 1937, launched an appeal for £100 to repair and keep the mill in working order. The repairs were carried out by Hunt of Soham in the following year, but during the course of the work a further weakness was found which necessitated more extensive repairs to be undertaken.

The mill finally ceased work in 1951 and was at first maintained by Mr Pegram. In October 1959 the Planning Committee recommended to the Cambridgeshire County Council that they should purchase the mill together with the land surrounding her. The Committee pointed out that although the mill no longer worked the present owner '. . . has made a very creditable effort to preserve this post mill. It is unlikely that he can continue its maintenance much longer. There is a very real danger that its condition will rapidly deteriorate resulting in its demolition.' However, nothing came of this and in 1963 the Chesterton Area Planning Sub-Committee engaged a millwright to inspect and report on the mill. He stated that considering the age of the mill she was in a very good condition and the Sub-Committee recommended that the County Council should purchase her. The mill was ultimately acquired and in 1966 restoration work was carried out by R. Thompson and Son of Alford, Lincolnshire. The whole mill was jacked up and the quarterbars and crosstrees removed. At this stage the mill was only propped up, and with the weather conditions rough, new crosstrees were laid and quarterbars fixed, the mill then being lowered back into position. One new stock was fitted with two new sail frames while the corrugated iron sheeting, which covered the breast, roof and sides of the second floor, was replaced with weatherboarding. The land surrounding the mill was attractively laid out and the mill has since been kept in excellent condition.

MADINGLEY MILL   NGR TL407595

This much-travelled mill, which stands close to the American Cemetery at Madingley, originally stood at Easton on a spot known as Mill Hill. She was at this time a simple post mill, and of considerable age, although the exact date of her erection is unknown. Sometime between 1840 and 1847 the mill was moved, about half a mile to the east, into the parish of Ellington by Mr Rowlatt, wheelwright from Easton. The mill was, at this time, modernized and reconstructed as a composite mill. The old body of the post mill was placed on top of a two-storey roundhouse, and a fantail fitted to the roof to drive a live curb. The common sails were replaced with patent ones and much of the old wooden machinery was renewed with iron machinery. Two pairs of over-driven stones were placed on a raised platform on the first floor of the body.

The mill, which was known as Red Mill from her original colour, was moved for James Measures, who carried on the allied trades of miller and baker in Ellington. On his death, about 1880, he was succeeded by his widow, Hannah, who carried on both trades until the turn of the century. The business carried on for a few years under the direction of Arthur Measures, but by 1910 the mill had ceased operations. The Measures family did not work the mill themselves, but probably employed a miller and inside the mill were two inscriptions—'W.F. 1828' (or 1848) and 'J.W. 1886'—which may have been the initials of past millers, while it is known that the last miller was a Mr Shadbolt.

The mill remained derelict, slowly deteriorating over the years, until in 1935 the mill was purchased by Colonel Walter Ambrose Harding of Madingley Hall. Anxious to replace an old post mill which once stood on the crest of Madingley Hill, he had for some time been searching for a suitable replacement. The former mill had ceased work in the 1870s, having been worked for many years by the Britchford family. The mill, which had four common sails and a thatched roundhouse, eventually collapsed in July 1909. On purchasing Ellington Mill, Colonel Harding consulted Charles Ison, a builder from Histon, with the result that Mr Ison dismantled the mill and re-erected her on her present site. The mill was considerably altered in the moving process, being converted to a Midland-type post mill, the body of the mill moving on rollers fixed to the body of the mill, on top of the single-storey roundhouse. The fantail was replaced with a tail pole with a wheel at the end, a ladder fixed, while two common and two single-patent sails were fitted instead of the four double-patent ones. The work was finally completed in June 1936, and within the mill there is a brass plate inscribed with the details of the mill's removal and re-erection. The mill, which now forms an attractive part of a residential stud farm, has been kept in good order by her subsequent owners, but she is now in need of some repair work.

OVER MILL   NGR TL381689

Overshadowed by the massive G.P.O. mast, the small tower mill at Over is the only windmill in the county still capable of and in fact still grinding grist. This is entirely due to the efforts of Graham Wilson, a Yorkshireman from Hull, who moved south because of his love of windmills. While working on Cattell's smock mill at Willingham, in 1960, he was able to purchase the mill at Over for £100. The mill at that time was in a poor condition, although the four sails remained perilously in position, as did the fantail. The cap, which had at one time a flat top which could be removed if required, was falling in and many of the interior timbers were rotten. Soon after purchasing the mill Mr Wilson began the work to avert further deterioration. He undertook the work single handed and within the first year had fitted a temporary roof over the mill, repointed part of the tower, replaced the decayed transverse and tail beams, rebuilt the fan frame and made new blades for the fan. This was followed in subsequent years by the rebuilding of the cap and gallery, new windows, replacement of much of the timbers within the mill, the installation of a pair of stones from the derelict mill at Upwell, and one pair of patent sails rebuilt and fitted. Finally, in October 1969, in a steady breeze the mill ground her first grist—some barley—for some forty years. Mr Wilson, who had by this time moved into the cottage adjoining the mill, hoped to work the mill commercially, but was unable to obtain sufficient work for this and so is now operating the mill more as a hobby. The restoration work cost Mr Wilson about £800, although he received a small grant towards the work from the Cambridgeshire and Isle of Ely Branch of the Council for the Preservation of Rural England. On 30th March 1974, he was presented, by Mr Rex Wailes on behalf of the Windmill and Watermill Section of the Society for the Protection of Ancient Buildings, with a Windmill Certificate in recognition of his efforts in restoring the mill.

The mill is reputed to have been built in 1860 for the small amount of £450, using materials from an old smock mill. If this is so she must have been built for Samuel Froment for he had purchased the mill in 1851 from Joseph Gifford. Benjamin and Wallis Cattell's names are found in old trade directories of the 1850s and 60s as well as the Froment family, but it is not now possible to determine which mill they worked. In 1875 the mill was purchased by Jonathan Parish, who also ran The Duke of Cumberland. On his death in 1894 the mill passed to his eldest son, William, by which time, according to the old deeds, a steam engine was also employed to assist in grinding. William Parish continued at the mill until 1912 when she was purchased by William Mustill, who remained there until she finally ceased work in 1929.

Cambridgeshire
WEST WRATTING MILL   NGR TL604510

In Cambridgeshire, at West Wratting, is the oldest-dated smock mill in the country with the letter 'W' and the date '1726' carved on the brake wheel. A small three-floored mill, with a circular brick base and an octagonal smock, she stands only 32 feet high and has been described as a '. . . small, cramped and ugly . . .' mill. The mill has many curious features and has evidently been much changed and adapted during her long life.

Little is known of the mill's early history, but by the 1840s George Poole was miller. He remained there until the early 1870s when the mill was acquired by George Gent who, in 1877, sold the mill, mill house and buildings to George Noble for £381. The Noble family came from Six Mile Bottom, where George also owned the old post mill. Later, he purchased four patent sails from a mill being demolished at Soham, and with these replaced one pair of common sails on each of his mills at West Wratting and Six Mile Bottom. From about 1880 the mill was leased to William Tredgett who, later, introduced a portable steam engine to assist in grinding. The engine drove an outside pulley which in turn drove, through a series of bevels, one of the stone spindles. The arrangement proved unsatisfactory and was later removed with the mill continuing to operate solely by wind. After George Noble's death, in 1903, the ownership of the mill passed to his son, George, who eight years later sold the complete property to Edward Purkins Frost of West Wratting Hall.

Mr Tredgett left the mill shortly afterwards, after which the mill was overhauled and let to the Farrow brothers. Up to the First World War they continued to grind animal feed and flour, but during the war the brothers abandoned flour-making although a little was again ground after the war. On the death of Mr Frost, in 1922, the estate was split up and sold with the windmill, house, stable, cart shed, granary and surrounding land being put up as one lot in an auction. The premises at this time were let to the Farrow brothers for the annual rent of £35. Whether the mill was sold is not clear, but the bidding is reported to have reached only £200. The brothers remained at the mill for two more years, but by this time the sails were in need of some repair which was considered uneconomic and the mill ground for the last time in October 1924.

In May 1934, efforts were made to preserve the mill. The Cambridge Branch of the Preservation of Rural England launched an appeal for funds, but nothing appears to have materialized and the mill slowly decayed. In 1960 Miss V. Z. Pumpei, the present owner, became anxious that the mill should not disappear like so many others had, and so she appointed an architect, Mr C. J. Bourne, to supervise the restoration

work. Although the work has somewhat altered the mill's appearance—the vertical boarding being replaced with horizontal boarding and the cap's shape altered—the work should ensure that the mill stands for many years to come.

WICKEN FEN MILL   NGR TL563707

On the National Trust nature reserve at Wicken Fen, stands the only surviving pumping mill of hundreds which controlled the water level of the fenlands and which have now been replaced by either diesel engines or electric pumping stations. This small four-sided smock mill originally stood in Norman's Dyke on Lapwing, the old turf diggings, near Harrison's Drove on Adventurer's Fen. Built as a skeleton mill in 1908, on the site of a previous wind pump, by Hunt's of Soham, she was weatherbonded in 1910 and continued to operate until 1938 when she finally became defunct, slowly becoming derelict.

In 1955 when an area of fenland in the nature reserve used in the propagation of wild seeds and plants was discovered to be running dry, it was decided to use a wind pump to pump water back into the fenland. The drainage mill at Adventurer's Fen was selected and, in that year, the Cambridge and Isle of Ely branch of the Council for the Preservation of Rural England decided to reconstruct the mill and move her, for the National Trust, to the new site one mile away. A scheme for her removal was devised with the expert advice of Rex Wailes and Mr Doran, Chief Engineer of the Great Ouse River Board. The work was financed by Lord Fairhaven, the chairman of the local branch of the Council for the Preservation of Rural England, with the construction work being carried out by Charles Ison, a wheelwright from the village of Histon, with the assistance of two apprentices, Leonard Froment and Robert Welford. Mr Ison dismantled the mill and re-erected her on the new site replacing all the original woodwork, but re-using all the original ironwork. New common sails and tail pole were fitted and the work finally completed in September 1956, when Lord Fairhaven performed the restarting ceremony. The mill was adapted to raise the level of water over the fenland and not for her original purpose of pumping water up from the field ditches into the main drainage dykes.

The mill at Wicken Fen is not typical of mills that once drained the fenland, for she is a small turf-digger's mill rather than a drainage mill. However, the remains of four drainage mills still survive. In Mildenhall Fen, Suffolk, stands Middle Mill which is now in the course of conversion into a dwelling. The age of the mill is unknown, but she appears on Lenny's Eau Brink map prepared in 1829–34. At Ugg Mere stands the hollow shell of the brick built Lotting Fen Mill, Built in 1872, she is of interest because she was one of the few mills erected with a scoop wheel capable of being driven by either wind or steam. She was last used in

1916. In Norfolk, at Nordelph, stands the remains of two mills which operated a double lift to drain part of Upwell South District into Well Creek. Both mills are now inhabited and both were apparently occupied by the millers who worked them.

Cambridgeshire
CATTELL'S MILL, WILLINGHAM NGR TL404697
The mill, situated in the village, was built for William Huckle in 1828—
a fact recorded on a stone above the door. The Huckle family were
prominent members of the village for many generations, and their names
can be found not only on the grave stones, but also on the tombs within
the church. The mill, which drove three pairs of stones, is unusual for she
is one of the few smock mills in the country to be built with a gallery
around her cap. By 1836, according to the Ordnance Survey map, there
were three mills in the village; the existing mill, a smock mill on the road
to Long Staton—known as Ingle's Mill which was demolished in 1956—
and another mill to the east of the village towards Belsar's Hill.

By 1841, according to the Tithe map, the mill was owned by Benjamin
How and was let to John Gleaves, a relation of Mr How. John Gleaves
also rented 34 acres of arable land and a house in the village from William and Benjamin How as well as owning 17 acres of arable land himself. The Gleaves family were also a large and prominent family in the
village, for the Tithe map indicates that no less than eight members of
the family were landowners, owning in all nearly 300 acres. By 1850
Joseph Gleaves had succeeded as miller, working the mill until the 1870s,
when he was followed by William Huckle Gleaves. In the late 1880s
steam power was introduced, and William Gleaves continued at the mill
to the mid-1890s when the mill was acquired by Charles Cattell.

At first Charles Cattell, whose father at one time worked a mill at
Over, went into partnership with a Mr Mustill, but by 1900 Mr Cattell
had taken complete control. Although steam power was dispensed with
on Charles Cattell's arrival, during the mill's hey-day no less than four
men were employed to work at the mill. A few years before the Second
World War Mr Cattell's son, Raymond, was taken into the firm and he
continued to run the business after his father's death in 1943. As trade at
the mill declined the firm transferred their interests towards the corn and
seed merchant business which is still operating in the village today. The
mill finally ceased grinding in the late 1940s and although Raymond
Cattell was anxious to repair the mill he was unable to find anyone prepared to undertake the work. Finally in 1956, Graham Wilson, who now
owns the mill at Over, undertook the extensive repairs with the assistance of Mr Cattell. In September 1958, it was reported that the mill was
once again grinding. The following year the County Council showed interest in the mill's preservation and an expert was appointed, but he, unfortunately, reported that the main timber structure was in such a poor
condition that he could not recommend her preservation. The Council
accepted this advice and no further action was taken. Although some
limited repair work was carried out by Mr Wilson in 1969, the mill is
once again in need of some repair work if she is not to deteriorate too far.

63

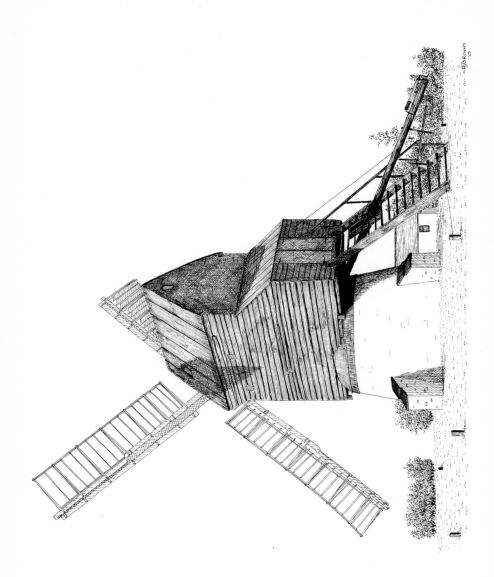

CAT AND FIDDLE MILL, DALE ABBEY   NGR 437398

Compared with other counties, Derbyshire has never had a great number of windmills, but the county has the distinction of having one of the finest post mills remaining in the country—Cat and Fiddle Mill at Dale Abbey. The mill, which is one of two post mills surviving in the county—the other being a mere skeleton at South Normanton, near Alfreton—is situated in a prominent position on the crown of a hill between the villages of West Hallam and Dale Abbey.

When the mill was built is unknown, but carved on the upper crosstree is the date 1788, which may be when the mill was constructed, although this could be earlier and probably succeeded an earlier mill or mills. The mill was originally built as an open-trestle mill, but in 1844 the present roundhouse was added, constructed of brick and local sandstone and whitewashed externally. The mill was not raised and to allow free access below the crosstrees, the floor was constructed below ground level. The mill was converted, like many others in the Midlands, into a Midland-type post mill. Repairs have been carried out over the years and in 1895 the lower crosstree was renewed, as too was the main post, which came from a mill at Colwick, and was put in by Bradford, a millwright from Grantham, Lincolnshire.

In 1912 the mill was acquired by the Stanton Ironworks Co. Ltd—now Stanton and Staveley—and has since been owned and maintained by them. In May 1943, in recognition of their efforts in maintaining the mill, the Company was awarded a Windmill Certificate by the Society for the Protection of Ancient Buildings. The Certificate was presented, on their behalf, by Rex Wailes to the managing director of the Company.

Who worked the mill early on is uncertain; in Kelly's Directory of 1855 only one miller is given, a David Cotton, but it is known that he was not at the Cat and Fiddle Mill, for later he is still given as miller together with John Porter, who is known to have been miller at this time. By the 1870s Stephen Smedley became tenant of the mill, together with Windmill Farm and began his family's long association with the mill. He was followed by his son, Stephen, who was later followed by his son, George. The mill worked regularly up until the end of the Second World War, when the drive to one pair of stones broke and, due to the shortage of labour, it was not repaired. The mill continued to operate until she finally ceased work in 1952, although still in working order, and on the death of George Smedley in that year the property was taken over by his widow, Marjorie.

HEAGE MILL NGR SO367507

Standing in a striking position on the brow of a hill overlooking the village of Heage, this tower mill, built of local stone, is undisputably the finest tower mill remaining in Derbyshire. Although the mill was probably built in 1850—a stone plaque by the side of the door is inscribed 'WM 1850'—there was a mill in the village many years before, for, in an advertisement in the Derby Mercury in 1816, a dwelling house, smock mill, and four acres of land were offered on lease in the village. The reference to a smock mill is of interest as this is the only reference to one in Derbyshire—a county of post and tower mills.

It was in 1850 that the Shore brothers took up residence in the village, purchasing the mill and trading as millers and grocers. Kelly's Directory of 1855 gives the brothers as Thomas, Isaac and John, but two years later another directory states that the firm was Isaac Shore and Company. The mill continued to grind until February 1894, when, during strong gales, the cap complete with her four sails were torn from the mill crashing to the ground. It was, at this time, decided to replace the four sails with six to increase the mill's power. The Butterley Company constructed a cross and windshaft capable of carrying six sails and George Chell, a millwright from Fritchley, fitted this together with the six sails, fantail and cap.

The firm continued to prosper for, shortly after the repair to the mill, the Shore brothers, Joseph and Isaac, employed no less than seven waggoners. The mill remained in regular use until 1916 under the supervision of Thomas Shore—son of Joseph and grandson of the founder—and was then used spasmodically until 1919 when the fantail was damaged.

The condition of the mill slowly deteriorated, although the remnants of the sails remained even after the mill was struck by lightning in 1961. In 1966 Mrs Harriet Wilders, who then owned the mill, applied for permission to convert the mill into a residence, but this was rejected by the County Planning Committee on the grounds that it would materially affect the appearance of the building. Instead they announced their desire to preserve 'the most complete surviving tower mill in the county' and negotiations commenced between the owner and the County Council. A preservation order was later placed on the mill, and in 1968 the mill was finally acquired by the County Council. The restoration work was commenced the following year with the fitting of a new cap, while internally repairs were carried out to the top floor. This was followed in the spring of 1972 with the making and fitting of six new sails followed, shortly afterwards, with the construction of a new fantail assembly.

AYTHORPE RODING MILL   NGR TL590152

In the centre of that area of Essex known as the Rodings, is an old post mill which stands proudly overlooking the fields as she has done for over two centuries. The mill is the largest post mill remaining in Essex, having a body 12 feet by 20 feet and 45 feet high with a roundhouse 24 feet in diameter. The exact date of her erection is unknown for she contains no inscriptions on her timbers, but there are records of a mill standing there for several centuries. However, she does not appear on Bowen's map of 1749, but is indicated on the Barrington Hall Estate map of 1766 and also Chapman & André's map of 1777, so putting the date of the present mill sometime between 1749 and 1766.

In the early part of the nineteenth century the mill, mill house, and the 'mill meadow', to the east of the mill, were owned by William Eve, who also owned the mill lane and a cottage, at the end of this lane, which was occupied by William Clayton. Mr Eve died about 1845 for the Tithe map of that year states that all the property was owned by his Trustees. According to the trade directories subsequent millers were G. Harris (1846), Stephen Cressingham (1848 and 1850), Edwin Bennett (1866), James Webster (1874 and 1878), Charles Large (1882), and Thomas Belsham (1892) on whose arrival auxiliary steam power was introduced. He remained miller for about ten years before his sons, Ernest and Jack, took over running the mill for the next thirty years. At this time the mill was owned by William Caton, a local farmer, in whose family the mill has remained.

The mill was last operated by Jack Belsham in 1935 and two years later his brother, Ernest, died at the age of seventy-nine. In the following year the Essex County Council made a preservation order on the mill under the Town and Country Planning Act. In 1941 the County Council accepted a 99-year repairing lease on the mill, but little work was carried out until new stocks and sails were made in 1956. One sail was again damaged in heavy gales the following year and this was repaired a year later. An application was then received by the County Council for conversion of the mill into a dwelling but this was refused. The mill was repainted in 1966, when much of the timber framework which supported the fantail mechanism was replaced. In 1972 a report, indicating that the mill was in poor condition, was sent by the Society for the Protection of Ancient Buildings to the County Council which resulted, in March of that year, in repair work being undertaken by the Council which included a new pair of stocks and inside sails.

A few miles to the south-west of the post mill, at White Roding, stands a tower mill which has the distinction of being the last mill erected in Essex. She was erected by Whitmore & Binyon of Wickham Market, Suf-

folk, on the site of an old post mill blown down in 1877. The mill ceased work in 1931 when the miller's lease was not renewed. In 1970 a new aluminium cap was fitted by Philip Lennard & Vincent Pargeter making this mill once again a striking landmark.

BOCKING MILL NGR TL763260

A very fine post mill stands at Bocking, near Braintree. Although believed to have been built in 1680 the exact date is unknown, but she was not the first mill built in Bocking, for an entry in the Court Roll refers to one in 1405. There is also evidence that more than one mill has stood in the parish, for Chapman & André's map of 1777 shows two mills. The present mill was purchased, in 1829, by John English Tabor, when she stood in Windmill Croft about a hundred yards further down the hill. In the following year he bought the present site and had the mill moved bodily up the hill. The two storey roundhouse was built and the mill herself probably largely rebuilt. At this time the mill was probably worked by John Brown followed by William Dixon, who was also licensee of the Bull Public House, which, up to a few years ago, was situated opposite the drive to the windmill. Other millers included Patrick Green and Robert Rutland, James Hicks and finally Henry Hawkins who was the last to work her in 1912.

In 1929, through funds raised by Alfred Hills, Clerk to the Braintree Urban Council, the mill was restored and in December of that year was handed over by her owner, Mr Edward Tabor, to Bocking Parish Council. The cost of these repairs was £225. She was the first post mill in the country to be taken over by the local authority as an historical monument.

During the Second World War and in the post-war years the mill was neglected, so by 1956 she was in a sorry state. At this time Braintree Urban District Council asked if the National Trust would be interested in taking over the mill. The mill was then in a dangerous condition through the splitting of one of the main beams and the estimated cost of repairs was around £500. In the following year the mill was again examined and it was reported that she was in danger of collapse, but with the aid of a grant from the County Council the mill was shored up. By 1961 there was talk of the mill being demolished, but fortunately some councillors felt that she should be preserved and an appeal was launched for £2,500, with the Urban District Council promising a grant of £1 for every £1 raised. In 1964 the target had been reached and the restoration work was undertaken by F. M. Noble Ltd of Ongar. When the work was completed, in November 1964, the mill was re-opened as a monument and a small museum was established in the roundhouse. A committee was formed to run and maintain the mill. The mill has been restored wherever possible to her original working condition, but owing to the need to strengthen the structure it was not possible to put her into operation. When working the mill drove two pairs of French stones, but only the bed stones are now in position, and to reduce the weight on the structure the runner stones have been removed and placed against the roundhouse.

FINCHINGFIELD MILL   NGR TL686330

Finchingfield post mill stands to the north of the village green on an unusually high mound, largely artificial, some 20 feet above the road. She is
close to the road, with the miller's cottage to the front, giving a very picturesque appearance over the house tops of one of the most beautiful villages in Essex. The mill, which is the smallest in Essex, is one of four
which at one time stood in the village and was built about 1760. Inside
the mill are the following initials and dates; on the middle storey is 'W. A.
1760, W. G. 1760, W. S. 1773' and on the crowntree is a small figure of a
post mill and 'W. & S. 1777'. In the Ipswich Journal of November 1792,
the following mill appeared for sale:

> 'A substantial newly built Post Windmill in the parish of Finchingfield
> near Gt. Bardfield, Essex—with one pair of French stones and all going
> gears complete'.

This may well have been the present mill for she drove only one pair of
stones, which was taken out and sold when the mill became disused, and
does not mention the roundhouse which was not built until 1840.

According to the Tithe map of 1834 the mill was owned and operated
by Edward Letch who also owned the mill cottage and the timber building, which still exists, on the opposite side of the road. He was followed by
his widow, Mary, in the 1850s and about 1860 she was succeeded by her
son, Andrew Luke Letch. As the population of the village declined—
from 2,595 in 1851 to about 1,200 today—so to did the trade of the mills,
and in the 1860s the present mill ceased work with the Letch family
moving to a larger mill to the south of the village. This mill finally ceased
work about 1904 and was demolished a few years later. By 1930 the present mill was dilapidated and it was reported that it was 'doubtful whether
it will stand much longer'.

However, the mill survived until 1947 when she was purchased by Sir
John Ruggles Brise, of Spains Hall, and presented to the villagers who
repaired the mill by public subscription. The body was re-
weatherboarded, four new, short, dummy sails fitted and the mill
repainted all at a total cost of £120. In 1957 the mill was in a semi-
derelict condition and the Parish Council asked the County Council to
undertake responsibility for her preservation. On the recommendation of
the Planning Committee the County Council decided to accept the transfer and carry out the necessary repairs. At this time two sails were missing, and it was known that at least £500 would be needed for structural
repairs. In fact, after the weatherboarding was removed, it was found
that a substantial amount of the framework required replacement, the
oak windshaft and brake wheel were rotten, and most of the mill had to

be rebuilt. An iron windshaft was acquired from Toppesfield tower mill, two new pairs of sails were fitted and a ladder at the rear fixed, but the tail pole was not refixed. The mill was repaired and repainted in 1968 and again in 1974.

INGATESTONE MILL   NGR TL639008

When Mr R. F. Collinson purchased his house at Mill Green in the 1950s, he was unaware that he had also purchased a derelict post mill which was at the bottom of his garden. In September 1959, he decided to rebuild the mill which had by this time become almost a complete 'write-off'. A trained engineer, Mr Collinson began by photographing every part of the mill and also drew extensive plans for the reconstruction. He engaged the services of an Essex firm Messrs C. J. Smith of Abridge, who, like Mr Collinson, had never before worked on a mill. The mill was scaffolded up under the supervision of Tim Mangan, a representative of another firm W. & C. French, and at one period the 'whole structure hung virtually by a thread'. A nationwide search was made for timbers large enough for the work, and slowly new timbers were added. Four new sails were fitted, the body weatherboarded, the roundhouse repaired and painted, the roundhouse re-roofed, new doors and floors added, a new tail pole fitted and the mill put back into working order. Mr Collinson supervised the whole of the work which, although proving to be very expensive, was undertaken without a grant. The work was completed in the spring of 1960 and has since been maintained in excellent condition.

The exact date when the mill was built is unknown, for although there is evidence that a mill has stood at Mill Green for over four hundred years, she does not appear on Bowen's map of 1749, and it is not until Chapman and Andrés map of 1777 that the present mill is indicated. Also within the old mill there was, painted on the main post, the initials 'E.D.' above the date '1759' and it therefore seems likely that the present mill was built on or near the site of an earlier mill in 1759 for Mr Dearman, who is known to have been miller some years later. A well-constructed mill, the crosstrees and main post were described as 'beautifully shaped' being extremely low in the roundhouse, the butt of the main post being no more than 1 foot from the ground. The tail pole had a chain to which a donkey was harnessed to wind the mill. The sails, which almost touched the ground, caused the death of at least one person, for in the Parish Register of 1774 there is recorded that on 6th August of that year the burial of Francis Allen, a farmer, took place who was killed by a blow from the sails of Mr Dearman's mill. Some seventy-four years later John Dearman was known to have been the miller, and was probably the son of the Mr Dearman mentioned in the Parish Register. In the early 1850s Alfred Tuck took over the mill. He, like John Dearman, was also a farmer and later operated the Ingatestone Steam Mill. By 1866 James Nicholls was working the mill, remaining there for some thirty years, before being succeeded by Joseph Nicholls. He operated the mill for only a few years for she had ceased work by about 1900. The mill remained derelict until Mr Collinson rebuilt her in 1959.

MOUNTNESSING MILL   NGR TQ631980

A well-known landmark on the main road from Brentwood to Chelmsford, the mill stands on a small mound to the west of the village. The mill was built in 1807—the date carved on the crowntree—for Joseph Agnis on the site of an earlier mill which disappeared in the 1770s. This earlier mill was figured on Bowen's map of 1749 and also on a road map published in 1766 in the Gentleman's Magazine but she is not indicated on Ogilby's road map of 1772 while on Chapman & André's map of 1777 only a mound is indicated. The present mill remained in the Agnis family for her entire working life passing from Joseph, on his death in 1851 at the age of seventy, to his son, Joseph. He remained miller for over fifty years some twenty of which, up until the mid 1870s, he carried on the associated trade of baker. In the latter part of Joseph's life, Joe Doe was employed as miller and at this time Mr Agnis lived in a house in Thoby Lane which had, on one elevation, windows with slate instead of glass—a relic of the old window tax.

Joseph Agnis died aged eighty-eight at the end of 1906, and was succeeded by his nephew, Robert Agnis, whose father worked for many years the old post mill at Billericay. For some years the Mountnessing mill worked with only two sails, but in September 1914, two additional patent sails were added after which only animal feeds were ground. An additional pair of stones, worked by a petrol engine, were housed in a shed nearby. The roundhouse—which in fact is a polygon with sixteen sides—originally had a thatched roof, but in 1919, due to the problem of it harbouring rats, it was replaced by a boarded and felt roof. Robert Agnis worked the mill until his death in the 1930s when his widow, Emily, took over the business continuing to work the mill until 1937.

In that year, through the generosity of Lord Arran, the mill, together with the adjoining playing fields, were acquired by the Parish Council as part of the Jubilee celebrations. In June 1937, an appeal was launched, and in the autumn of that year repairs were undertaken by Christy & Norris, millwrights of Chelmsford. The work included the renewal of two sails, repairs to the weatherboarding and the repainting of the entire mill of which a third of the cost was met by the Essex County Council. The mill was, after the war, again repaired by the Parish Council, but shortly afterwards she was struck by lightning. In 1956 the County Council accepted ownership from the Parish Council and that winter the County Council fitted two new sails, repainted the mill and reglazed the windows. A new ladder was made in 1966 followed, in 1970, by two new sails made and fitted by the millwrights Lennard & Pargeter. In July and August of the following year the roofs of the mill and roundhouse were

covered with aluminium sheeting. The sails were again damaged in the
gales of February 1973, these being repaired in August of the following
year by R. Thompson & Son of Alford, Lincolnshire, when the mill was
again repainted.

STANSTED MILL   NGR TL510248

The mill, which is about 65 feet high, was built in 1787 by Joseph Linsell together with the mill house. The mill was first designed to carry spring sails and to adjust the spring a stage was provided, which was later removed when patent sails were fixed.

In 1807 the mill was auctioned and bought by Mr Chaplin. By 1848 Thomas Sworder owned the mill and in March of that year Edward Hicks, the miller, reported that a sail had 'blown off and her back broken'. Mr Sworder replaced these with a pair of patent sails. In 1860 Mr Hicks suggested to Mr Sworder that the mill be demolished and a steam mill installed, but fortunately this was not carried out. In 1887 the mill was again put up for auction, being this time acquired by James Blyth—later the first Baron Blyth of Stansted Mountfitchet. She was let to Messrs Hicks, millers and maltsters, who had worked her intermittently from 1844 until 1910. The second Lord Blyth sold the mill, but bought her back to prevent her being pulled down. In 1929 he approached the Society for the Protection of Ancient Buildings about the mill's preservation, and work commenced in 1934 when extensive repairs to the structure and machinery were carried out. On completion of the works the mill was conveyed for the benefit of 'the inhabitants of Stansted', the Rex Wailes and the Parish Councillors being appointed co-trustees.

During the early part of the Second World War the mill was severely damaged by a storm, and, by the end of the war, the condition of the mill had deteriorated. In 1949 a Windmill Restoration Committee was formed to raise money so that essential repairs could be undertaken. Later the cap was covered in aluminium at a cost of £300. Part of the cost was met from a grant from the Pilgrim Trust and the Essex County Council on the understanding that the mill be scheduled as an Ancient Monument. The Windmill Restoration Committee was, in 1960, reformed as the Stansted Mountfitchet Windmill Committee being a committee of the Parish Council, and a further appeal for funds was made. The Pilgrim Trust made a further donation and money was also received from the Historic Buildings Council, the Society for the Protection of Ancient Buildings, Saffron Walden Rural District Council, and from the general public including people in Australia and Canada. The work was let in the summer of 1966 to F. M. Noble, Ltd of Ongar. It included replacement of the sail and fantail, repointing and repair of the brickwork, repairing the plasterwork and the external painting. However, much of the internal repairs were undertaken by volunteer members of the Stansted Windmill Association. The total cost for the work was £2,487 and was finally completed in September 1966, when the mill was floodlit for a public reception.

STOCK MILL NGR TQ698989

There was at one time three mills—two post and one tower—standing together on what was once Stock Common, and these were the last of several mills built in the village of which the earliest is recorded in 1437. A mill indicated on the Common on Bowen's map of 1749 is in much the same place as one on Chapman & André's map of 1777. This same mill is shown on a map of 1779 for the estate of the Rt Hon. Robert Edward Lord Petre, indicating that the owner occupier was William Moss at a rent of £2. 2s. 0d. per annum. William Moss constructed the present tower mill beside the old post mill in 1799–1800. At this time another post mill was situated at the eastern end of the village, in a field adjoining the Bakers Arms or the Jolly Miller's Beershop as it was then known. By 1841 the two mills had passed from William Moss, Senior, to his son, William, for, according to the Tithe map of that year, both mills were owned and occupied by William Moss, Junior, while the surrounding 'mead' was still owned by his father, who also owned a number of the adjacent cottages. In 1845 William Moss, Junior, purchased the other post mill in the village from her miller, George Threadgood, and the wooden structure was transported on a horse-drawn trolley to her new position beside the other two mills. It is stated that the miller was all the while in a state of fear in case the load should topple.

William Moss, Junior, retired about 1860, but whether he retained ownership of the mills is unknown although he was described as a landowner. He was succeeded as miller, for a few years, by John Pertwee who in turn was succeeded by the Clover family—first by Joseph and then, on his death in the 1890s, by his widow, Mary. It was during the Clover's period as millers, about 1890, that the two post mills were demolished because, it was reported, 'there was not sufficient wind for them' although it is more likely that there was not sufficient work for them. William Mayes succeeded Mrs Clover as miller, and on his arrival auxiliary steam power was introduced. On his death in 1920 the mill was put up for auction being advertised as a '. . . substantially built windmill with portable steam power (driving three pairs of stones) . . .' and was purchased by Mr Spurling, a farmer, for £1,040. Frank Semmers followed by Sidney Semmers ran the mill until 1937.

In the following year the Essex County Council made a preservation order, but due to the war nothing more was done. The mill suffered through the depredation of trespassers and the curiosity of sightseers until, in 1944, she was purchased by the County Council in order to preserve her as an ancient monument. In 1956 a new stock and a pair of sails were replaced by R. Thompson & Son of Alford, Lincolnshire, while general repairs and repainting have since been carried out at regular intervals by the County Council.

THAXTED MILL   NGR TL609309

A few hundred yards south-west of the fine church at Thaxted is the town's sole surviving windmill. The mill was built in 1804 on the site of Thaxted Church Mill—a medieval post mill—by John Webb, a prominent person in the town. A landowner, he not only owned Park and Borough Farms but also other property in the town itself. It was from his lands that the clay was dug for the manufacture of the bricks for the massive tower, and it is reported that the timber used in the mill was cut from the farms. By 1827 his son, John Webb, Junior, was described as miller and in 1834 on his father's death, the mill together with other property was left to him. The remaining property was left to Robert Franklin— John Webb, Senior's son-in-law. John Webb, Junior, was also a man of some wealth for not only did he own the mill and Borough Farm but also four houses, thirty-two cottages and other odd parcels of land within the town. John Webb employed two millers to operate the mill—Joseph Thurgood and Robert Lowe—and on his death, in 1863, he rewarded each for their service by leaving them nineteen guineas. The remainder of his estate was left to his brother-in-law Robert Franklin who, in the same year, let the mill, together with a barn in Fishmarket Hill, to Arthur William Clarance for the annual rent of £45.

Upon the death of Robert Franklin in 1869 the mill passed to his son, Thomas. In about 1888 Robert Lowe—John Webb's former employee—became miller and it was in this year that the mill became in need of major repairs. Walter Gentry, a millwright from Braintree, was employed to undertake the work, but when presented with the bill of £200. 2s. 11d. Thomas Franklin thought it 'an outrageous amount to pay', and when finally paying up he commented that if the mill was sold tomorrow she would 'not make the money it has cost me'. In that year Mr Franklin also paid out £64. 10s. for materials and three years later had to pay a further £87. 7s. to Mr Gentry for more repairs. When Mr Franklin died, in 1907, the mill was put up for sale, but was later withdrawn continuing to be let to Harry Lowe, who had taken over as miller in the late 1890s at a yearly rent of £35. The mill finally ceased work in about 1910 after which Mr Lowe continued to trade as a corn factor.

The mill slowly decayed until in 1932 the Thaxted Civic Trust acquired her, repairing the structure so that she could be used until the 1950s by the Scouts and young people. When the Civic Trust wound up in the early 1950s the mill passed to the Parish Council. In 1964 the Thaxted Society was formed and later the Essex County Council included the building in the town's conservation area. In 1970 a Windmill

Committee was formed and a public appeal was launched. Grants were
received from the Department of the Environment and the County
Council and the work was commenced in 1973 by Philip Lennard who is
undertaking the work in three stages.

DANZEY GREEN MILL, AVONCROFT MUSEUM OF BUILDINGS

NGR SO954683

This post mill, which now stands preserved at the Avoncroft Museum of Buildings, originally stood in an open field in the hamlet of Danzey Green, near Tanworth-in-Arden, Warwickshire. It is known that a mill has stood at Danzey Green for over three hundred years and this, the last mill, was built about 1800. The mill, which was in the Munt family for over one hundred and thirty years, appears to have ceased work in the 1880s for the Ordnance Survey map of 1886 shows the mill as being 'disused'. By about 1910, according to an old photograph, the mill already showed signs of decay with the sails partly broken. The mill deteriorated unchecked until, by the 1960s, she was on the point of collapse. At this time she was described as an 'impressive timber skeleton' and all that remained was the framework of the body and the stocks, together with the roundhouse walls.

In 1969 negotiations commenced between the mill's owners, Alne Estates of Tanworth-in-Arden, and the Avoncroft Museum. Following consultations with windmill experts and the owners it was decided to dismantle the remains of the mill, including the brick roundhouse, and restore and reconstruct her on the Museum's ten-acre site at Bromsgrove. The mill was photographed and in July 1969, she was dismantled. The work was undertaken by two engineers and windmill enthusiasts, Michael Field and Nigel Fredrick, together with a group of volunteers. The timbers were carefully labelled and a crane employed to remove the windshaft, brake wheel and remains of the sails. By November 1969, Mr Greiner, the Museum's carpenter, had repaired the timbers of the body's framework which was then reassembled on the ground. In March of the following year the roundhouse was reconstructed using some seventy per cent of the original bricks. A main post from another mill, that had collapsed, was used with relatively little modification and the body framework, the restored windshaft and brake wheel were raised. Four new sails—two common and two spring replacing the original four common ones—were made by Derek Ogden and fitted at the end of August, when the floors and weatherboarding were completed. Following an extensive search new millstones, obtained from Weston Jones Watermill, Staffordshire, were fitted.

The work was completed in the summer of 1971, and this typical Midland-type post mill is the only post mill in working order in the West Midlands. The cost of the work was in the region of £5,500, with the Victoria and Albert Museum, the Ministry of Public Buildings and Works, the Muntz Charitable Trust and the former owners contributing over half of this. The remaining amount being raised by public subscription.

85

Cromer Mill   NGR TL304286

Cromer Mill, which dates from about 1720, stands on an artificial mound where a mill has stood, it is believed, for over six hundred years. During the first half of the nineteenth century the mill was run by the Munt family being succeeded by Ebenezer Boorman, who combined the trade of miller with that of iron founder. After his death, first his wife, and then his son, Ebenezer, ran both businesses until the turn of the century when Ebenezer gave up the mill to form an engineering, ironfounders, and blacksmith firm in the village. Ebenezer Boorman was followed as miller by Joseph Ponder Scowen, who continued until shortly after the First World War, when she was finally taken over by Richard Michael Hull.

The mill continued to work by wind until 1926 when a gale caused one stock to fall, damaging the roof of the roundhouse as it fell. After this the mill became 'headsick' so the remaining sails, which would not pass the roundhouse, were subsequently removed. The mill finally ceased work in about 1930, after which she was almost demolished and disposed of for the value of her timber. However, in 1938 through the initiative of Captain Barry some repairs were carried out, assisting her to withstand the ravages of time.

By the 1960s the mill had badly deteriorated; the timbers suffering from both beetle and dry rot. However, partly because she formed a conspicuous landmark, and partly because she was the only surviving post mill in the county, widespread concern was felt about her future. In 1966 The Hertfordshire Building Preservation Trust, under the chairmanship of Mr E. A. Williams, decided to set aside the sum of £800 from their funds towards the ultimate cost of restoration. An appeal was launched for £3,000, the estimated amount to restore the mill completely. By 1967 £2,800 had been raised, sufficient to commence the rebuilding of the body, and the contract for this first phase was let to J. A. Elliott, Ltd of Bishop's Stortford. By the autumn of 1967 the first phase had been completed, including the repair of a decayed internal beam together with the replacement of the weatherboarding. During the year an appeal was made to the County Council, who responded in 1968 with a grant of £1,200 towards the scheme. The next phase of the work was placed with E. Hole & Son, millwrights of Burgess Hill, Sussex. This work included the making and fixing of the exterior ladder, fantail, stocks, and sails which were finally fixed in position in 1969. The work was carried out under the direction of the Hertfordshire Building Preservation Trust and the County Planning Department. After the work was completed, George Turner of Cottered, who owned the property, conveyed the mill and site free to the Hertfordshire Building Preservation Trust.

SKIDBY MILL   NGR TA021334

This mill, a prominent local landmark on the eastern flank of the Yorkshire Wold, is the sole surviving windmill in full working order north of
the Humber. Built in 1821 by Gartons of Beverley for William Watson
she was eventually acquired, in 1854, by Joseph Thompson in whose
family she has remained ever since. Joseph Thompson came from a milling family for his father, Leonard, worked a windmill at Hessle. The
business expanded until, in 1878, he took his eldest son, Leonard, into
partnership and moved to new premises in Hull. Although the firm continued to expand at Hull the old windmill in Skidby, and later the
watermill at Welton, remained an important part of the firm.

The windmill continued to work by wind until September 1947, when
the breast beam was found to be defective. To reduce the weight on this
beam the shutters were removed from the sails, but milling was continued with the aid of an electric motor. It was not until July of the following year that a suitable beam was found to replace the defective one,
and this was fitted by R. Thompson & Son of Alford, who later replaced
the shutters in the sails and repaired the fantail. Although the mill was
never again worked commercially by wind, she was kept in excellent
repair by her owners, and, in 1962, R. Thompson & Son was again
brought in to replace a sail damaged in a gale earlier in the year.

In this year J. G. & B. Thompson were taken over by the Weston
Group of Companies, who continued to work the mill—producing meal
for feedstuffs—until 1966. The following year J. G. & B. Thompson, on
behalf of the new owners, approached the Beverley Rural District Council, and the Council agreed in principle to accept responsibility for the
mill's future preservation. It was stated that about £2,000 had been
spent on the mill's upkeep over the previous four or five years. It was not,
however, until November 1968, that the mill was finally presented by
Eric Thompson to the Council. In the following January the Council
accepted a tender of £519 for the treatment of woodworm and mealworm
in the mill, half of which was contributed by the East Riding County
Council. This was followed, in July, by repair work and repainting which
amounted to £725.

In September 1970, Beverley Rural District Council decided to convert part of the surrounding building into an agricultural museum. After
deciding to spend £2,500 on repairs and improvements the County
Council decided to contribute half towards the cost and a further grant
of £850 was received from the Department of the Environment. By the
end of 1973 further repairs were needed to the sails but to assist with this
and other costs a second grant of £1,350 was made in November 1974, by
the Department of the Environment.

WALTHAM MILL   NGR TA260034

The mill at Waltham, the last to be built in Lincolnshire, was built by
Saunderson of Louth, on a site formerly occupied by two post mills. The
first of these was blown down in 1744 and the second mill, built to
replace her, was blown down during a gale in December 1873. This mill
had for many years been worked by the Little family—first William and
for the last few years by Germain. The present mill was built in 1879–80,
for about £500, in the traditional Lincolnshire style, but much of the
main timbering was secondhand with the main shears coming from a
demolished church. These timbers are too short for the job intended, and
so the weatherbeam is supported in front of them on iron plates. The mill
is unusual for a Saunderson mill in that she does not have the characteristic hand-forged, wrought-iron balcony or stage.

In 1882 Thomas Rodgers came to the mill to begin the family's long
association with her. He came from Cleethorpes Mill, where he had been
an apprentice, and rented the mill from John Saunderson. In 1900 Mr
Saunderson sold the mill to Benjamin Crow, and it was not until some
years later that Mr Rodgers acquired her. During the First World War
the mill lost one of her sails and the opposite sail was removed to balance
her. The mill has remained working with four sails ever since as, at the
time, the timber needed to replace it could not be obtained and so the
work was never done. An unusual occurrence happened during the war
when Mr Rodgers was accused of signalling to the enemy at night when
the sails passed the windows. He was taken before the magistrates but the
case was dismissed. He continued to work at the mill until his death in
1938 when his son, George, took over. He continued until his retirement
in 1950 when his son, Thomas, who had worked at the mill most of his
life, succeeded him. The mill finally ceased work by wind in 1962
although she continued to operate occasionally by electric engine.

By 1966 concern was expressed about the future of the mill, and in
December of that year the Waltham Windmill Preservation Society was
formed. Work was undertaken by R. Thompson & Son of Alford, to
replace the decayed cap and fantail, while the Society arranged for the
mill to be repainted. A grant of one third of the cost was obtained from
both Lindsey County Council and the Ministry of Public Buildings and
Works. In 1971 the Rodgers Trust, owners of the mill, declared their
willingness to sell and the Grimsby Rural District Council agreed to
negotiate the purchase of the mill and lease her to the Society. In March
1972, the Council made an offer of £2,000 for the mill, but this was rejected, by the owners, as being inadequate. Nothing more happened until
1974 when the Preservation Society, who had already spent £2,000 on
the mill, requested that Cleethorpes District Council again re-open negotiations with the owners and this was agreed.

WRAWBY MILL   NGR TA025088

Commanding a position on an escarpment of the Lincolnshire Wolds is
Wrawby post mill—the sole surviving post mill in Lincolnshire and
Humberside. The exact date when the mill was built is unknown, but it is
thought to be between 1760 and 1790. In 1800, according to the Wrawby
cum Brigg enclosure award, she was the property of Cary Elwes who at
that time owned most of Brigg, Wrawby and district. In 1810 Simon
Rusling was miller and other millers included James Coulbeck, and Mr
Mackman. Mr H. Andrew succeeded Mr Mackman as tenant in 1885
and continued to work her until the 1900s.

In 1910 the two main sheers broke and the Elwes Estate agent
suggested that the mill be demolished. She was, however, purchased by
Mr R. Andrew, father of the last miller, who repaired the mill to working
order. In 1917 the remaining pair of common sails were removed and
replaced by spring sails obtained from the dismantled mill at Laceby,
near Grimsby. H. & W. Andrew succeeded their father and continued to
work the mill until the loss of one sail in 1940 finally brought the mill to a
standstill. The business continued until the late 1940s by the use of an
oil-driven pair of stones, which had been installed in 1914 in the warehouse opposite.

The mill slowly deteriorated and attempts to restore her in the 1950s
failed. By 1961 the mill was on the verge of collapse and when, in March
of that year, the property again changed hands the new owner, Mr M.
O'Connor, requested permission to demolish the building as he considered her unsafe. A society was formed, under the leadership of Captain J. Elwes and Jon Sass, with the support of Mr O'Connor, in an effort
to restore the mill. A fund was started and grants were obtained from the
Ministry of Public Buildings and Works, Lindsey County Council, Brigg
Rural District Council, Captain Elwes and the Lincolnshire Association,
while the Lindsey County Council also made in addition a loan of
£1,000. Details of the mill were recorded, and in 1962 the internal
machinery, sails and the body were removed while the roundhouse was
repaired. Two new crosstrees and four new quarterbars were made, from
two oak trees given by Lord Yarborough, to replace the existing ones
which were badly decayed. Messrs Scarborough & Ferrier of Cleethorpes
constructed a new body which was assembled on site and lifted, by crane,
and fitted on to the re-erected post. During the winter of the following
year two sails, taken from Halton Holgate Mill, were repaired and modified. The internal machinery was re-installed during 1964–65 and one
pair of stones dressed and refitted. Two secondhand sails were fitted in

1965, the petticoat and ladder made and a tail pole fitted. On 18th September 1965, the mill was officially set in motion grinding her first bag of corn for twenty-five years. Two new sails have since been made and the second pair of stones reinstated.

Isle of Wight
BEMBRIDGE MILL   NGR SZ639875

The only surviving windmill on the Isle of Wight is at Bembridge. The mill was built, upon the orders of the Lord of the Yaverland Manor, in about 1700, when she was not situated at Bembridge, but on Binbridge Isle, now a name of the past due to the reclamation of Brading Harbour between 1894–97. Built of local stone the original mill had a thatched roof, but about 1720 this was replaced with one made of wood. The earliest positive date in the mill is 1746 which was found on one of the strings of the ladder from the machine to the stone floor. This ladder was replaced, but the section containing the inscription—'E. Beker 1746 AC'—has been preserved. On the woodwork of the tentering gear can be seen another date which, although not very distinct, may well be 1701 and possibly the date of the mill's construction.

The mill was in continuous use, grinding flour, bran and cattle feed, until the 1890s after which she ground only the latter. The mill finally ceased work after the harvest of 1913 when she was owned by Alfred Morris, who farmed both Stanwell and Mill Farms. Gradually she decayed and became infested with woodworm and death-watch beetle until, in 1933, the Society for the Protection of Ancient Buildings launched an appeal for £100 to carry out the necessary repairs. A local committee was formed and restoration work was undertaken in 1934–35. Unfortunately no provision was made for the mill's endowment and no income was provided for her maintenance. After ceasing work the mill was used as a cow shed and a store until, during the Second World War, she was taken over by the Army and Home Guard as a headquarters and observation post.

After the war the mill was in an almost derelict state. One pair of sails had disappeared—struck by lightning during the war—and of the remaining pair little survived, the roof leaked, doors were broken, floors and ladders rotting. When Mr Morris died he left the mill to his niece, Mrs E. Smith, who, early in 1957, offered the mill, together with the adjoining land, to the National Trust. In 1958, the Island National Trust Properties Management Committee launched an appeal for funds and with over £1,000 raised by public subscriptions the work was put in hand, under the direction of the Trustees, in 1959. The sails were made by Mr F. Cheverton from a drawing by Mr R. C. Durden. The mill became the property of the National Trust in 1962 and opened to the public. The original stones had been removed in the 1920s, but fortunately these were replaced by two pairs taken from the old tide mill at Wootton Bridge, when this was demolished in 1963.

95

CHILLENDEN MILL   NGR TR268543

Standing alone in a field in open country near Eastry is Chillenden post mill. The mill is the only open trestle-type post mill remaining in Kent and although built in this old style she was not, in fact, built until 1868 when the modern tower and smock mills were firmly established. Built to replace an older post mill, which is shown on Robert Morden's map of 1695, she incorporated material from an old mill, for a seventeenth-century date has been discovered inside the mill. This white-painted mill was one of the last mills erected in Kent, and was certainly the last post mill to be built in the county.

The mill was first worked by Messrs Haywood & Cage, described as 'millers and farmers', followed by William Hopper Bean. Later Mr A. Laker operated the mill, and was succeeded by his nephew Mr N. W. Laker who had assisted his uncle for many years. Mr Laker was only thirty-one when the mill finally ceased work in 1949 although, for many years, the mill had been only grinding oats for cattle.

The mill lost a sail in a gale in 1949, and soon fell into disrepair with the tip of one sail resting on the ground apparently supporting the 'head sick' mill. In 1950 the Wind and Watermill Section of the Society for the Protection of Ancient Buildings, and the Committee for the Preservation of Rural Kent became anxious over the future of the mill. After a report on the mill and an estimate for her repair, the Section suggested that a local fund-raising appeal be launched. The appeal raised enough by 1955 for the mill to be rendered weatherproof, but in the intervening years further deterioration had occurred. Finally it was decided that Kent County Council should take over the mill, and subsequently the owner, Brigadier E. J. L. Speed of Knowlton Court, Eastry, sold the mill with about three-quarters of an acre of land at market value to the Kent County Council so that the mill could be restored and preserved. He was unable to make a gift of the mill for she was part of property held in trust, but he donated £100 towards the cost of the scheme to maintain the mill.

The mill was restored, for a sum of £728, as a landmark, but the small barn, which stood nearby, was demolished and some of the machinery from the mill removed. The brake wheel has been strapped with iron to the cross beam so the sails will not turn, and the ladder bolted to concrete blocks so the body will never again face the wind but will continue to face southwards. The shutters of the sails are skeleton frame, with the canvas removed, to reduce wind resistance, so avoiding too much maintenance. It is a pity that such a fine mill will never again face the wind or the sails turn.

97

UNION MILL, CRANBROOK   NGR TQ779359

Described by many as the finest smock mill in the country, she dominates
the skyline of the small town of Cranbrook. Her white-painted body,
standing on a black tarred brick base, reaches a height of 72 feet and with
her patent sails and fantail is an impressive sight.

She was built in 1814 by James Humphrey, for a Henry Dobell, at a
cost of £3,500. Dobell operated the mill for about five years, but after he
became bankrupt the mill was taken over by his creditors who formed a
company to run the mill—hence the name Union. This company continued to operate the mill until 1832 when she was bought by George and
John Russell. In 1840 Medhurst, the Lewes millwright, erected four
patent double sails together with a new windshaft and in the same year a
fantail was erected by George Warren of Hawkhurst. Forty years later
the present stage was erected by Warren, replacing a former timber one.

The mill was run successfully by the Russell family for many years.
John was followed by his son, Ebenezer, who in turn was followed by his
sons, Hugh and Caleb, and finally in 1918, by John, Caleb's son. The
fantail and shutters had been removed in 1912 and so, at first, John ran
the mill with four common sails and no fantail. In 1920 he brought four
common sails from Sarre Mill and fitted one pair, converting them to
spring sails. A new fan was made in 1921, by William Warren of Hawkhurst, being fitted by John Russell, who, in the following year, fitted the
remaining sails and converted all the sails to patent ones. Just before the
Second World War, in 1937, Mr Russell made and fitted one new sail and
in 1946 rebuilt an old one. However, in 1950 the mill finally stopped
working by wind when one of the stocks became decayed. Two years later
an electric motor was installed and the firm continued to operate using
this source of power.

The mill soon became in need of repair, and the Society for the Protection of Ancient Buildings appealed for funds for restoration, enabling
work to be finally put in hand in 1958. This work, carried out by Chris
Bremer, a Dutch millwright, included the installation of new steel stocks
imported from Holland. These differ from the usual form in that the
shutters are fitted directly to the stocks. However, during the restoration
work further timbers were found to be defective necessitating their replacement. The mill was left in skeleton condition during 1959, but the
following year Chris Bremer returned to fit two new cant posts, replace
the weatherboarding and fit the shutters to the steel stocks. The total cost
of the work was £6,000. Kent County Council, who now own the mill,
have maintained and run the mill at intervals to keep her in working
order. John Russell, who had maintained the mill for so many years, died
in 1958, three days after restoration work commenced.

99

HERNE MILL   NGR TR185665

This black tarred smock mill is situated on the brow of a hill overlooking the village of Herne. She was built in 1781 by John Holman, when working for Sweetlove, the millwright of Wingham, to replace an old post mill that had stood there early in the sixteenth century. In her early days the sails of the mill came almost to the ground and with the trees close by much of the wind power was lost. So, in 1858, the whole of the wooden structure of the mill was bodily raised and two floors of 18 inches-thick brickwork was built up underneath. The raised mill was then able to take advantage of the prevailing south-west winds.

The first owners of the mill were Lawrence and Sons. They handed the mill over to Thomas Wootton in 1879, who with his brother, John, successfully operated the nearby Chislet Mill. From Thomas ownership passed to his son, Frank, and has remained in the Wootton family ever since, being at present owned by Messrs Wootton Brothers the two sons of Frank—R. C. & E. E. Wootton.

The mill ran for many years on two sails and in 1930 money was raised locally to purchase a new pair but it was then found that the cap would not bear the extra weight and the money had to be returned to the subscribers. In 1931 the cap became stuck and on examination by Holman Brothers it was found that a new worm was required and that the wooden cogs to the curb needed replacing. In February 1935, the Society for the Protection of Ancient Buildings launched an appeal for £115 as part of the framing was in need of repair and the sails were decayed. The work was carried out by Thomas B. Hunt, millwright of Soham, Cambridgeshire. Unfortunately it was essential that the other pair of sails were replaced, and the money was raised by the Society for the Protection of Ancient Buildings, Trinity House and Princess Marie Louise, the Duchess of Kent.

The mill continued to work by wind until the 1950s, although she carried on working by electricity, when negotiations began for the preservation of the mill. In 1956 the Society for the Protection of Ancient Buildings carried out a few repairs as a temporary measure. By 1957 it was agreed that the Kent County Council would accept the mill as a gift, keeping the mill in repair, and granting the present owner a 999-year lease at a nominal rent. The cost of the restoration was estimated at £2,000. However, the Herne Bay Urban Council declined to increase their contribution towards the repair beyond £200 and finally the County Council abandoned the scheme. Finally the Herne Society was formed, and, with money raised by them and with contributions from the County Council, work was at last started in 1971 by the firm of Lennard & Pargeter. The estimated cost to restore the mill to full working order was then £6,000.

101

Kent
DRAPER'S MILL, MARGATE   NGR TR363700
This smock mill, in the middle of Margate, has over the last few years
been restored to full working order. The mill, which like many mills in
Kent is owned by the County Council, is the last windmill in Thanet—an
area once famous for its barley and windmills. She was built sometime
between 1840 and 1847, for although she does not appear on the Tithe
map of 1840, in Kelly's Directory of 1847 J. Banks is named as miller.
The mill was built by John Holman, millwright of Canterbury, and is
one of three mills which stood at one time in the area. Next to the present
mill was a smaller smock mill called Little Draper's Mill—moved from
Barham in 1869 and dismantled in 1929—and close by a five-sail tower
mill, used for pumping water, known as 'The Pumper'. According to W.
Coles Finch in his book *Watermills and Windmills* there was a mill on the
site in 1695. J. Banks was succeeded in running one or both mills by F. &
E. Darby, Thomas Ind and finally Thomas R. Laidlaw. She last worked
by wind in 1916 when a gas engine was installed to carry on. In 1927 the
sails were thought to be unsafe and these were removed together with the
fantail, although she continued to work, by the gas engine, until 1933
after which she became derelict.

By 1965 the mill was in a poor state and there were plans to demolish
her to provide space for new homes. Interest, however, was aroused and
the Draper's Mill Trust was formed under the chairmanship of Mr R. M.
Towes, headmaster of the adjoining Junior School. With the aid of
grants from the County Council, Margate Urban District Council and
the Historic Buildings Council the committee succeeded in rasing £2,500
towards the cost of the restoration. In 1968 the Kent Education Committee acquired the site, finally averting demolition by agreeing an
exchange of land as an alternative building site. Within one month of the
acquisition by the County Council repair work was commenced with F.
J. Doughty Ltd, a local building firm, undertaking the repairs for a total
cost of £2,000. The work entailed the renewal of some of the structural
members and fan staging, and the replacing of the weatherboarding to
the body and cap. In the winter of 1970 the fantail was added by the millwrights Pargeter & Lennard, and in December of the following year
these two erected one pair of sails. Later the stage was fitted—this was
originally intended for Barham Mill which was burnt down in 1970—
and in the autumn of 1974 the other pair of sails were fitted. Inside the
mill there are many exhibits from Barham Mill and the old post mill at
Ash, which collapsed in a gale in 1955 when negotiations were taking
place, with the County Council, for her restoration.

103

MEOPHAM MILL   NGR TQ639652

One of the finest mills in the county is situated close to the village green at Meopham. The mill was built in 1801 from, it is believed, an old broken-up battleship from Chatham dockyard for the three Killick brothers. The three brothers, who also carried on business as millers at Strood, walked daily a distance of eight miles from their home town to Meopham Green, and constructed the mill as a 'model mill'.

The mill was owned by James Killick, but on his death in 1889, at the age of ninety-seven, the business passed to his son, Thomas, who shortly afterwards sold it to John Norton, whose brother, Tannor, worked the mills at West Kingsdown. In 1895 John Norton took his nephew, William, son of Tannor, into partnership and the firm of J. & W. Norton was formed. The mill, which was unusual for making her own electricity, last ground flour about 1914, but continued to grind animal feed by wind for another thirteen years. During this period she worked, for many years, on two sails supplemented by an oil engine from 1927. When William Norton died after the last war his son, Leslie, who had joined the firm on leaving school, continued to work the business alone until, in the early 1950s, he was joined for a short while by Mr V. R. Moarby and a limited company J. & W. Norton (Meopham) Ltd was formed. The firm continued to operate until 1965 crushing and grinding animal feed.

In 1958 Leslie Norton approached the Kent County Council for assistance in her preservation, and in the following year, after an inspection by the County Architect, they decided to proceed with her restoration. The Council acquired, by deed of gift, the land on which the mill stands from Mr Norton, and then leased the mill back to him for 999 years. The restoration work was commenced in May 1962 by E. Hole & Son of Burgess Hill, Sussex, at a cost of £4,375 which included recladding the structure and renewing the balcony, floors and staircase. In mid-October of the same year the four sails each 27 feet long and weighing 17 hundredweights were fixed. Later that month the work on the mill was completed. After the death of Mr Norton, in 1967, the lease of the mill was put up for sale and a Trust was formed to acquire the lease for the mill together with the yard. With the assistance of the Meopham Parish Council, the Meopham Society, and a grant from the Pilgrim Trust sufficient money was raised to purchase the mill. A number of the derelict buildings on the site were demolished, the mill cleaned from top to bottom, and the site grassed and fenced. The mill was finally opened to the public for the first time in July 1971. The mill is subject to an annual inspection while the sails are rotated a quarter of a turn every three months.

ROLVENDEN MILL   NGR TQ838315

The date of erection of the mill at Rolvenden is uncertain, but there is no doubt that a mill has been on this site for many hundreds of years. There is in existence documentary evidence of a mill house standing here in 1556 and a mill must have stood at that time. The mound, on which the present mill stands, is probably even older than this. A mill at Rolvenden is shown upon Symondson's map of 1596 although this is not the present mill for no mill is shown on either Morden's map of 1680 or Bowen's map of 1736. Harris' map of 1719 indicates a mill on the present site and it is, therefore, probable that another mill occupied the site sometime between 1680 and 1736. A mill is shown on all County maps after 1736 and, therefore, the present mill was probably constructed sometime after this date. The earliest date in the mill is 1772, carved on the framing inside the mill, while further carvings are 'E. W. & H. Allen 1828', on the main post, and on the side framing is the name 'E. Witt' with a faded nineteenth-century date. These names are probably past millers.

The miller in 1834 was Thomas Record followed in 1839 by Richard Reeves who was, at the same time, also running the mill at Benenden. The mill and mill house were at this time owned by Thomas Gybbon Monypenny, a member of a local landowning family. Reeves was followed by George Bridge, Laurence Foster, John Greenhill and finally Horace Dunk, who on giving up milling in 1883 turned his attention to farming although continuing to live in the mill house. After this the mill was let to Mr Collins, who owned the mill at Sandhurst, but he closed down the mill at Rolvenden in order to keep the trade for his own mill. In 1885 two sails were removed while the roundhouse, which was of wood, was pulled down for firewood during the First World War. The ladder hung tenaciously until 1917 when it finally collapsed.

Although some repairs were carried out in the 1930s, by the 1950s the mill was in very poor condition, with the timber to the first floor, framing to the breast and much of the weatherboarding needing replacing. All that remained of the other pair of sails was the stock and fragments of the sails. Restoration was commenced in 1956 by R. Thompson & Son of Alford, Lincolnshire, under the supervision of Rex Wailes. The work was financed by Mr & Mrs H. A. Barham of Saxbys, as a memorial to their eighteen-year-old son, John, killed in a road accident the previous year. A stone is let into the side of the brick roundhouse in memorial. The work included the repair and renewal of the internal framework, renewing the weatherboard, fitting new sails and building a brick roundhouse, but the ladder was not replaced.

ST MARGARET'S BAY MILL   NGR TR363435

This mill is situated high on the South Foreland Cliffs at St Margaret's-at-Cliff, overlooking the English Channel, in the private grounds of Windmill House. She was built for the sister of the late Sir William Beardsell. Sir William, a lover of windmills, had the idea of taking down a windmill he particularly liked and reconstructing her as part of the house near his own home which was built around the old South Foreland Lighthouse. He bought a mill, but this was found unsuitable for the move and although he searched the country he could not find another. Eventually his architect suggested building a new smock windmill and this was finally agreed. The house was started in 1928 being built by William Cocks & Son with the mill constructed by Holman Brothers, the famous millwrights of Canterbury. She was the last mill to be built in the county. Although not built primarily as a windmill it worked in every respect despite the sails being of smaller design than usual. No grinding stones were provided, for the owner hoped to use the power to generate electricity for the house and the mill started working in this capacity in June 1929, and continued to work until the onset of the Second World War. The specialized equipment for generating electricity is housed within the lower floors of the smock, although the dynamo was removed during the war. The brick base is an attractive furnished addition to the adjoining house linked by passage. The mill originally had a creosoted body with the cap, sails, fantail, base and stage painted white.

The mill became a local beauty spot and was a landmark for mariners in the Channel. During the Second World War she became empty until a special branch of the W.R.N.S. moved in to occupy the building. German documents captured after the war included many long range photographs of St Margaret's Cliff with the windmill plainly visible.

After the navy moved out the mill remained idle until, in 1958, she was repaired and redecorated. In 1969 the mill was repaired and overhauled by the millwrights Philip Lennard and Vincent Pargeter. This included the rebuilding and replacement of the fantail, stage and gearing, the repair to the sails, and repairs and reboarding to the cap. The mill was then substantially in working order and with some of the shutters fitted to the sails the mill was once again capable of working, and was regularly set in motion by the owner. The mill was later struck by lightning causing damage to one of the whips which was later renewed. In 1972 the house and mill, which is included in the Statutory List of Buildings of Special Architectural or Historic Interest, was again sold for a sum in the region of £60,000.

109

STELLING MINNIS MILL   NGR TR146465

The smock mill at Stelling Minnis is one of the few remaining mills in the
county to be in full working order and has the added distinction of being
the last mill to work commercially by wind. She was built for George
Goble in 1866, by Thomas Richard Holman, millwright of Canterbury,
on the site of an old post mill. On Mr Goble's death, in 1878, the mill was
acquired by Henry Davison in whose family she remained for nearly one
hundred years. Some eighty years ago, when Mr Davison was attending
his sister's wedding, the mill was not only struck by lightning, but also
tail-winded and it is reported that the cap was lifted up from the body of
the mill although fortunately it was not removed. In the early part of this
century auxiliary power was added, and the four sails were shortened to
clear the new engine house, built next to the mill, and presumably at this
time the stage was constructed. Flour was last ground at the mill in 1907
and finally ceased to work by wind in 1925, when the milling operations
were carried out by a Hornsby paraffin engine. By the 1930s the four
sails and fan were described as 'broken and in poor condition'.

In 1935 the mill was restored to working order, and she reverted to
wind power using the oil engine only when there was insufficient wind.
The repair was financed by Miss Hilda Laurie in memory of her brother,
Ronald Macdonald Laurie, and a plaque inside the mill records this fact.
In the following year a certificate was presented by the Society for the
Protection of Ancient Buildings to Miss Laurie, and this also hangs
within the mill. Another interesting item, is the record of the stone dressing undertaken by a T. Crittle at the end of the last century and pencilled
on the cant and adjoining timbers on the second floor.

In 1940 the mill passed to Mr A. Davison. At this time the timber
sill—which is only just above ground level—was replaced as the old sill
had decayed due to rising damp and gnawing rats. In May 1951, the mill
lost two of her patent sails during a gale, but although shortly afterwards
negotiations were commenced between the County Council and Mr
Davison for the replacement of these sails, the plans did not materialize
and the work was not carried out. Some repair work was carried out by
Vincent Pargeter in the 1960s, before he became a professional millwright, and later, when partnered by Philip Lennard of Essex, he undertook repairs to the curb and cap. Mr Davison retired in the autumn of
1970 shortly before his death. At the end of 1973 Kent County Council
decided to spend £5,000 on repairs to put the mill, once again, into full
working order, but it was not until 1975 that the mill was finally
acquired. Work was commenced at the mill by the East Kent Mills Group
which was formed in 1975 to preserve the water and windmills in the
area.

111

Kent
WEST KINGSDOWN MILL NGR TQ582623

West Kingsdown smock mill, standing close to the main London to Dover road, is a conspicuous feature of the landscape with her black octagonal weatherboarded body and white sails and fantail.

The mill was originally situated at Chimham's Farm, Farningham, and is thought to have been built at the beginning of the nineteenth century for she was first depicted on the early maps of that century. The mill, while at Farningham, was operated by the Collyer family, W. Moore and finally by the Norton family. Ten years after the death of David Norton his son, Tanner, purchased the mill and moved her to the present position. The re-erection was carried out by George Paine at a cost of £800 and a foundation stone, built into the brick base, bears an inscription 'Minnie Louisa Norton, April 21st 1880'.

At this time there was also a post mill standing there, which had been in the Norton family for many years. In May 1909, this mill was destroyed by fire when permission was given for a road roller to draw near the mill, and a spark from the engine set fire to some straw which spread to the mill. The post mill, being all timber, was soon destroyed.

The smock mill passed to Frank Norton, on the death of his father, Tanner, and he carried on the business for several years until finally the mill was sold to Mr Cork, the last miller. The mill ceased to work in 1928 and in the following year Mr Cork sold the mill to Mr Hankin, but she never worked again. A sail was damaged in a gale on Christmas Day, 1929, and the fan blown down in November 1930.

The mill then became derelict and by the 1950s she was in a very poor condition. In 1955 plans were made to repair the mill at an estimated £1,250, but nothing came of this. In 1958, after several months of negotiations, the Kent County Council agreed to accept the mill as a gift, but the County Council granted the owner, Douglas Heaton, a long-term lease and he was not required to enter into any covenant with regard to repairs. The repairs were at that time estimated at not less than £1,800 and regarded to be very urgent if the structure was to be preserved. The restoration, however, was completed at the end of April 1960 at a cost of £4,400 of which Dartford Council contributed £400. The work was carried out by R. Thompson & Son, millwrights of Alford, Lincolnshire. The main gearing was removed some years ago and was not replaced, but the three pairs of millstones were set in position.

WITTERSHAM MILL   NGR TQ913273

This mill, also known as Stocks Mill, stands in the grounds of a private house, in the hamlet of Stocks, not far north of the boundary between Kent and Sussex. Inside the mill, carved on the main post, are three sets of dates and initials—R.V. 1781, R.A. 1785 and I.B. 1790—the first of which is thought to be the date of erection. This is substantiated by the fact that the mill is not included on Andrews, Dury and Herbert's map of 1769 or on Hasted's maps of 1778 to 1801. She is, however, known to have been in existence in 1792 for within the mill is a copy of the entry in the Book of the Royal Exchange Assurance stating that the mill, mill house, and the personal property of the miller—a Thomas Howards— was insured for a total of £500 at a premium of £1. 9s. 6d. with the value of the windmill stated as £250. There was also an older mill standing at Wittersham, to the north of the village, which appears on all county maps from 1736.

According to the Wittersham Tithe map of 1838, both mills were run by Richard Parton—probably related to the Parton family who worked the nearby mill at Woodchurch—owning the older mill but renting the present mill, together with 'Little Field' and 'Great Meadow', from Henry King. Other millers known to have worked the mills were Robert and Peter Parton, G. Burch, H. S. Hyland, S. Birch and, towards the end of the last century, Thomas Collard who was the last miller clearly indicated as operating both mills. The Stocks Mill ceased work in the early part of this century, but the older mill continued until between the two wars when she was finally demolished.

The mill was maintained in good repair by her owners, and in 1955 a report was sent to the Kent County Council by her owner Admiral Sir Edward Parry informing them that there was considerable local interest in the preservation of the mill. He added that a committee of influential local residents had been formed, and that he was willing to transfer the mill to a holding trust or public body, subject to certain conditions. However, the County Council decided that, provided that sufficient local financial support was forthcoming, they would consider an application for a contribution towards a satisfactory scheme for preserving the mill. In 1958 four new sails were made and erected by a local craftsman, Mr H. Payne. The money for this work was raised by the Windmill Preservation Committee with assistance from the County Council. In 1968, after one of the stocks broke in a storm, further work was carried out by Derek Ogden, in consultation with the Society for the Protection of Ancient Buildings, and financed by an appeal among local inhabitants with another grant from the County Council. The mill is now inspected yearly by Mr Ogden and the sails turned through ninety degrees to relieve strain.

115

Lancashire
LYTHAM MILL   NGR SD371270

There has been a windmill at Lytham since at least 1327, when in a deed
the Prior of the Benedictine Priory granted part of the waste land to John
de Bradkirk, his wife and to their son for his lifetime, provided the corn
grown there was ground at Lytham Mill. Later, in the seventeenth century, a document shows a post mill between Lytham Hall and St
Cuthbert's Church. By 1787, according to William Yate's map of Lancashire, there were two mills in this area, on a site now enclosed by Hall
Park.

The present mill, which stands in a picturesque setting on the famous
green overlooking the sea, was not built until 1805, when Richard Cook-
son applied to the Squire for a plot of land on which to erect a windmill.
In the building he incorporated materials and machinery salvaged from
other disused Fylde mills—the date 1762 found within the mill has
misled many about the mill's age. The mill, which has a cellar and four
storeys with walls 5 feet at the base, originally had common sails, but
these had, by 1870, been replaced with patent ones.

At least two fatalities have occurred at the mill. In 1877 a man, visit-
ing the miller, was struck by a sail and was so seriously injured that he
died a few hours later. The other occurred in 1909, when a schoolboy, on
a trip from Manchester, caught hold of one of the revolving sails and was
swept up until at the top he lost his nerve. He fell to the ground and was
killed instantly.

The mill continued to operate until New Year's morning 1918, when
she was ravaged by fire and never worked again. The mill was gutted,
machinery fell through the floors, grain was destroyed and, according to
one report, timbers from the sails were scattered beyond St John's
Church. The mill was then purchased by the Local Council and in 1921,
on the amalgamation of Lytham and St Annes, it was decided to restore
her. New dummy sails were erected, but no machinery was installed and
the total cost of the work was £1,114. After this she was used as a café, an
electric sub-station and the headquarters of the Lytham Motor Boat
Club, the Lytham Sea Cadets and finally the Ribble Cruising Club.

The mill is maintained by the Council and in 1963 the interior was
found to be decayed with rot. Experts were called in, and much of the
flooring was replaced with new timbers, while the remaining timbers
were treated against further decay. This work was followed by further
restoration work carried out by R. Thompson & Son of Alford, Lincolnshire. At the beginning of 1975 four new common sails, complete with
sail cloths, were fitted and, as an attraction at the holiday resort, it is
intended that these should, from time to time, turn in the wind.

117

Lancashire
MARSH MILL, THORNTON   NGR SD335426
There is no doubt that this mill at Thornton is the finest mill in the
North-west. She was built in 1794 for Hesketh of Fleetwood—over the
door is a stone tablet inscribed 'Bold Fleetwood Hesketh 1794'—by
Ralph Slater, the Fylde millwright, who also constructed the mills at Pill-
ing and Clifton. The mill, which stands about 70 feet high and 34 feet
diameter at the base, was originally built with common sails, but these
were later replaced with patent ones and this could have been in 1895
when the original oak windshaft was replaced with the present cast-iron
one. The oak windshaft was apparently sold to a company formed to
make relics from the timbers of the Fonderait, Nelson's flagship, which
had been wrecked at Blackpool.

The mill was first operated by Samuel Thomason and subsequently by
his son Richard, and later by James Tyler who sold her in 1896 to Messrs
Parkinson to Tomlinson, corn millers of Poulton.

The mill continued to operate until 1922, although for some years she
only ground animal feeds. The mill remained idle for a few years before,
in 1928, being converted into a café. Later she became a factory and a
store. In 1944 the owner of the mill came forward with a plan to restore
the mill and hand her over to the National Trust as a memorial to his son
killed in the war. No more, however, was heard of the plan. The mill was
put up for sale by auction in 1954, but little interest was shown for, including the auctioneers and newspapermen, the attendance barely
reached twenty. After this there was pressure on the local Council to purchase the mill and preserve her.

Finally, in 1957, the mill was purchased by the Thornton and Cleve-
leys Urban District Council for £1,200. The money for the purchase of
the mill and the adjoining house came from a Ministry of Local Government loan sanction. Soon afterwards the Council carried out renovations
and repairs to the mill at a cost of £750. After the work was carried out, it
was proposed to open the mill as an historical showplace, but unfortunately in December 1962, two sails were blown off in a gale. In
November 1963, a restoration fund was launched, but in the following
January one of the remaining two sails was blown down. Restoration was
finally commenced in August 1965, by R. Thompson & Son of Alford,
Lincolnshire. The estimated cost was over £3,000 and included the fitting of a new fantail, four new sails, repairs to the stage, partial renovation of the machinery and other minor alterations and repairs to the
interior and exterior of the mill. In 1968 a grant of £1,000 was received
from Lancashire County Council towards the cost and the District
Council decided to allocate £250 each year towards repairs. Internally
the work has been carried out by Walter Heapy with the assistance of a
volunteer work party.

119

KIBWORTH HARCOURT MILL   NGR SP688945

Amid the rolling countryside between Leicester and Market Harborough is Leicestershire's sole remaining post mill. The mill, which stands some 400 feet above sea level, is situated in the grounds of Windmill Farm and is believed to date from the early part of the eighteenth century, although a mill was known to be on the site early in the seventeenth century. The earliest inscription, carved on the main post, is 'Daniel Hutchinson Miller 1711' and this may be the date of her erection. The mill was worked for over fifty years by the Smith family first by Thomas, then Charles and finally by Mrs Elizabeth Smith—probably the widow of Charles—who continued to work the mill until about 1916. At this time the following notice was to be seen inside the mill:- 'Table of fees in lieu of toll to be taken at the mill—for wheat 9d per bush; for all other grain 6d and to be conveyed to and from the mill by the employer.'

The mill slowly fell into disrepair until in 1936, following concern over the mill's future, a local fund was started to enable the mill to be repaired and preserved. The mill was at this time owned by Merton College, Oxford, who conveyed her to a group of local trustees acting in conjunction with the Society for the Protection of Ancient Buildings. The mill was repaired and slightly modified and four new sails fitted. In 1966 a preservation order was made by Leicestershire County Council on the mill which, by this time, was again needing major repair work. The owner, Brian Briggs, who had been keeping the mill in repair for many years, was unable to find the considerable sum needed for this work. In 1970, during International Conservation Year, a new committee was formed with the idea of restoring her. Five new trustees were appointed and a millwright was consulted, who estimated the cost for restoration at £3,500 and an appeal was launched. Mr Derek Ogden, millwright of Great Alne, Warwickshire, undertook the work which was somewhat complicated and prolonged by the fact that much of the external framing was found to be decayed. Some of the restoration involved making good work undertaken in 1936. The repairs to the sails were a major job, for the two remaining sails needed renovation while a new pair of common sails were made and fitted. Inside the mill the floors were renewed and the two pairs of millstones—one Derbyshire peak and the other French burr—were reset. Some of the gearing was replaced, while the windshaft was retained though it was altered. A new tail pole was fitted, to replace one removed in 1936, and a new ladder at the rear added. The final cost of the work was over £4,000 of which the Leicestershire County Council provided a grant of £2,000, and another £2,000 from the Department of the Environment, with the balance coming from the Windmill Preservation Trustees.

ALFORD MILL   NGR TF457766

Alford, up to 1931, had the unusual distinction of having a four-sailed, a five-sailed and a six-sailed mill at work in the town. The four-sailed mill stood near the station, the six-sailed mill in the yard of the Half Moon, while the five-sailed mill still stands, complete with all sails in full working order, at the east end of the town, and is the last windmill to work commercially in Lincolnshire. She was built by John Oxley—a local millwright from Alford and founder of the present firm of R. Thompson & Son who has done so much in maintaining the mill in her present excellent condition—with ironwork by William Tuxford, millwrights and engineers of Boston. A bakery was built at the side of the mill and, as is common practice in Lincolnshire, both these allied trades were carried on at the premises.

After a number of bakers and millers the property came, at the end of the nineteenth century, to Harry Hoyles who first rented them before finally purchasing them some years later. Harry Hoyles came from a milling family and learned the trade at his father's mill—Friskney Low Read Mill—which had been in the family since before 1842, while his brother Joseph worked the mill at Maltby-le-Marsh for many years. Harry Hoyles, who was for many years a local councillor, died in 1949 after being baker and miller in the town for over fifty years. He was succeeded by his elder son, Walter, who continued to run the business with the assistance of his two brothers, Arthur and Winton. The three continued to trade until 1955, when they were finally forced to close down as they could no longer compete with the large bakery firms while, on the milling side, more and more farmers were installing hammer mills and grinding their own animal feed.

The buildings remained empty until November 1957, when they were purchased by Charles Fredrick L. Banks, a miller from Kirton Lindsey, who learned his trade at his father's mill at Sturton by Stow. At first he was going to remove the sails and refit them on his mill at Mount Pleasant, which was powered by diesel and electricity, but following an appeal by the Society for the Protection of Ancient Buildings he agreed to allow the sails to remain, and also to repair the mill so that she could once again be put to work. The repair work was undertaken by R. Thompson & Son assisted by Mr Banks and was finally completed in the spring of 1958. On 21st April 1958, Mr Banks was presented, by Rex Wailes on behalf of the S.P.A.B., with a Windmill Certificate in recognition of his efforts in conserving the mill. In December 1970, Mr Banks decided to sell the mill, being prepared to consider offers in excess of £6,000. His reasons for selling were the long distance from his home and the high cost of maintenance, but no offers were received and Mr Banks

continued at the mill. At the end of 1973 Mr Banks announced that the cap and sails needed replacing. The estimated cost of these repairs was £13,860, and a fifty per cent grant was obtained from the Department of the Environment leaving Mr Banks to raise the remaining amount.

MAUDE FOSTER MILL, BOSTON NGR TF332447

The sole surviving windmill of several which once stood in Boston, she stands in the Skirbeck Quarter overlooking the Maude Foster Drain from which the mill derives her name. Next to the Stump—Boston's famous church—the mill is the main feature of the skyline. She was built in 1819 for Thomas & Isaac Reckitt—Isaac being the founder of that famous firm of that name—by Norman & Smithson of Hull, who agreed to undertake all the '. . . wood, iron, brasses, millstones, glazier work and labour, all outside woodwork to be painted with three coats of paint, the whole finished in a good workmanlike manner . . .' with the exception of the attractive yellow brick tower, for the sum of £1,200. The business soon expanded for, in 1821, a bakehouse was started and this was followed two years later by a mill for cement manufacture and the installation of a steam engine costing £300. In 1835 a bone mill was added when bones were bought, crushed and ground for fertilizer.

In 1835 the partnership between Thomas & Isaac Reckitt was dissolved and the following advertisement for sale, in the Stamford Mercury of the 16th March 1835, gives an excellent description of the mill at this time:

'. . . newly erected Corn Wind-Mill, seven stories in height, having patent sails that work three pairs of French stones, with an excellent Grannery and dry-kiln sufficient to contain several hundred quarters of wheat, large Dressing and bolting machines, Jumper, etc. thereto adjoining and belonging. Also a building used as a bakehouse, attached to the above described premises, with two extensive ovens therein. A Cart shed and a three-stalled stable, and every other requisite convenience for carrying on trade . . .'.

The mill was subsequently sold to George Cooke of Digby, Lincolnshire, who after a few years sold her to Jonathan Dent, who had endeavoured to purchase her from Thomas Reckitt some years previously. Thomas Reynolds was miller for some years and in 1853 George Spurr took over, being described as a 'corn miller, oil miller and bone crusher', with other premises in Market Place and High Street. He remained at the mill for over twenty years until 1878, when he was succeeded by Jessop & Sons who also dealt in corn, cake and artificial manures. The premises were also used, for sometime, by Charles Jessop, builder and contractor. The last person to operate the mill was Alfred Ostler who took over the mill from the Jessop family in 1914. On Mr Ostler's death the mill passed to his executors.

In 1953 the mill was restored as a landmark with money provided from a charitable trust established by the late Albert Reckitt, a grandson of Isaac the original owner. The work was carried out by R. Thompson & Son of Alford, Lincolnshire, for the total cost of £790.

DOBSON'S MILL, BURGH-LE-MARSH   NGR TF503649

There are two mills standing at Burgh-le-Marsh—the empty shell of a former four-sailed mill standing on the hill and the preserved five-sailed mill in the hollow. The five-sailed mill—still known locally as Dobson's Mill after the last miller—was built about 1833 by John Oxley, the millwright from Alford. He built many mills in Lincolnshire, including the tallest mill in the county at East Kirby, near Spilsby, before he lost his life in a fall from a mill at Barrow-on-Humber. He was followed at Alford by Edward Wheatcroft and in 1877 by Robert Thompson, founder of the present firm of millwrights in Alford. The mill, which was built for Agar Jessop, is said to have the best-built tower in the county and originally had a stage around the mill and common sails. About 1870 the common sails were replaced with patent ones and the stage removed. At this time the three pairs of stones—two peak and one French burr—were also lowered one floor to make the work easier. About 1880 Robert Barker took over the mill and bakery and on his death, some ten years later, was succeeded by his widow, Susan, who ran both businesses until they were finally taken over by Martin Barker.

In 1929 the Barker family's association with the mill ended after fifty years when the mill was purchased by Frank Dobson. He was miller at Grebby, near Scremby, where his father, Edwin, had also been miller. Frank Dobson ran both mills for some years continuing to trade under the name of E. Dobson & Son before he finally concentrated his efforts at Burgh-le-Marsh. When Frank Dobson retired from the mill his son, Edwin, took over although he continued to own the property. Edwin ran a successful bakery business employing a miller to work the mill. The last miller employed there was George Bamber, who left in 1963 leaving Mr E. Dobson to carry on with this side of the business as well. In 1964 Mr Dobson gave up the business and the property was sold.

The new owner stated that he had no intention of operating the mill, and in February 1965 Lindsey County Council started negotiations with him to buy the mill in an attempt to ensure her preservation. Later that year the County Council put a building preservation order on the mill while negotiations were under way. These were finally completed in July, when the Council agreed to pay £5,650 for the mill, house and outbuildings. Following the purchase, the County Council accepted Skegness Urban District Council's offer of an annual contribution towards the repairs and maintenance and asked Spilsby Rural District Council for a similar offer. The future care and management of the mill was put in the hands of the Sandhills Sub-Committee. Various restoration work was put in hand and the old bakehouse, together with the outbuildings, were altered to form the Windmill Restaurant which was leased the following year to Peter Chambers from Bratoft.

127

Heckington Mill   NGR TF145436

Beside the railway station at Heckington is the only surviving eight-sailed windmill in the country. Originally a six-sailed mill, she was built in 1830 by Michael Hare, and was worked for over forty years by the Nash brothers—Sleighton & Joseph—until in 1890 she was, it is believed, burnt out. Another report states, however, that the cap and sails were blown off in a whirlwind and the sails crashed in a field on the opposite side of Great Hale Road narrowly missing the signal box.

Later the tower was purchased by John Pocklington who also bought, for £100, Tuxford Mill, Boston, which stood on part of the site required for the construction of Boston Docks. This mill had been built in 1813 by William Tuxford, the engineers, millwrights and millers of that town and Mr Pocklington dismantled the mill and transferred the cap, sails, fantail and interior to his mill at Heckington. The work was carried out by Mr Pocklington with the assistance of John Hobson, a local millwright from Heckington, with the five-ton windshaft being lowered, transported and re-erected on successive Saturdays in the snow. When he was fifteen John Pocklington's father had died leaving the family in penury. Within two years of erecting the mill he had established a thriving bakery business and by 1896 had increased his business activities to include those of timber, cake, corn and coal merchant. He was always proud of the fact that the mill drove a circular saw, which was used to cut up elm boards out of which coffins were made for the village. Later he took his sons into the firm and launched out into farming.

The mill finally ceased work in 1943 on the death of Mr Pocklington, and remained empty until 1953 when it came to Kesteven County Council's notice that the owner, John Pocklington, was proposing to remove the sails. The Council, anxious to preserve the mill as a 'monument to the period of windpower', purchased her for £2,000. The repair work, which was undertaken by R. Thompson & Son of Alford, included the fitting of four sails—two each from the mills at Old Bolingbroke and Wainfleet. On 31st July 1954, to mark their appreciation of the efforts of the County Council in preserving the mill, the Society for the Protection of Ancient Buildings presented them with a Windmill Certificate. The presentation was made to the Chairman of the Council, Sir Robert Pattinson, on behalf of the Society by Rex Wailes. In the summer of 1969 the mill underwent further extensive repairs after being described, at a County Council meeting, as being in a dangerous condition. This work was again carried out by R. Thompson & Son at an estimated cost of £2,729. The work included the replacing of four sails, producing an exact replica of the fantail and the re-painting of the mill. The mill was struck by lightning in the late spring of 1972 when the sails were damaged, these being subsequently repaired by R. Thompson & Son.

129

TRADER MILL, SIBSEY NGR TF344510

This mill at Sibsey was built in 1877 on the site of an old post mill by John Saunderson, millwright of Louth, whose firm was famous throughout the country for their large multi-sailed mills, and who had the distinction of not only building the last corn mill in Lincolnshire, at Waltham, but also, in 1892, the last corn mill in England at Much Hadham, in Hertfordshire. The Trader Mill, which is considered to be the finest example of Saunderson's craft and has their characteristic wrought-iron railing around the stage, is built in the traditional Lincolnshire style using bricks made from clay obtained from the nearby Trader Pits. There is a story that the carters who carried the bricks were in the habit of calling at the Trader Inn, which, at one time, stood on the road opposite the mill, and on the day that the brickwork was finally completed they took their beer mugs and had them bricked into the final course of brickwork.

The mill was first worked by Clapham Mawer until soon after the First World War when she was purchased by Tommy Ward. He was a great character who took pride in maintaining his mill in first-class condition and was never prouder than when talking about her. His first love was steam, for his family were steam cultivator proprietors. The mill remained in excellent condition until 1950 when she lost a sail, but by taking off the opposite one Tommy Ward was able to continue to work her until his death in 1953. After this the mill was purchased by Mr R. H. Crawford, a farmer from Frithville, who shortly afterwards sold her to Mr W. Pannell, who worked her until 1955, before finally she was re-purchased by Mr Crawford after which she ceased work.

In November 1963, an attempt was made by the Lincolnshire Local History Society to restore the mill to her original condition. An estimate of £3,500 was obtained from R. Thompson & Son, the Alford millwrights, which was mainly for the repairs to the cap—which was very dilapidated—the renewal of four sails and two new sails. An appeal was launched to raise the money; the Ministry of Public Buildings and Works promised to contribute £1,000 towards the cost and it was hoped that Lindsey County Council would make a similar contribution. However, it was not until 1970 that restoration work was finally commenced, being commissioned by the Department of the Environment although the building was still owned by Mr Crawford. The work was undertaken by Sibsey contractors F. Evison, who had been doing repairs on the mill for twenty years, and included carefully cutting out and replacing over 6,000 bricks on the tower. R. Thompson & Son were employed to repair the cap and make and fit the six new sails which were hoisted and fitted on 28th September 1970, under the supervision of Jack Thompson who was, at that time, aged eighty-four.

131

ARKLEY MILL   NGR TQ218953

Arkley Mill is generally thought to have been erected at the beginning of
the nineteenth century, but she is not shown on either A. Bryant's map of
Hertfordshire of 1820/21 or on the first Ordnance Survey map of 1822.
The first indication of the mill's existence is on the Shenley Tithe map of
about 1841, where it is stated that she was owned and occupied by James
Whitehead for whom she is thought to have been built.

By 1854 Everett Whitehead had become miller and was, presumably,
James Whitehead's son. He did not work the mill for long, but retained
ownership of her, first leasing her to William Hyde and later to Frederick
Edwards. In 1878 Mr Whitehead was living at Potter's Bar, Middlesex,
and was stated to own one acre of land in Hertfordshire—the windmill
and surrounding land—with another twenty-five acres in Middlesex. On
his death, in 1896, at the age of seventy-one, the mill was sold by auction.
Frederick Edwards continued at the mill until about 1900 when he was
succeeded by his son, Noah. Steam power had been introduced by 1881
and an old photograph, dated about 1890, indicates that the mill had, at
this time, two common and two patent sails. Shortly after this the mill
lost one pair of sails, but although replaced the same thing happened
again a few years later with the result that the mill continued to work
with two common sails. When there was no wind, in the evening, Noah
Edwards would sit on the fan stage and play his fiddle.

In 1916 the working life of the mill ceased, and she fell derelict with
the result that by 1929, when purchased by Colonel William Booth, the
mill was in a ruinous condition. The following year an estimate was
obtained from Hunt Brothers of Soham, Cambridgeshire, for the restoration of the mill. The work included the renewal of two sails, the cap,
gallery, fan stage and fantail for the cost of £156. However, with the replacement of all windows and ladders, the final cost was over £300 and a
substantial contribution was received from a member of the Society for
the Protection of Ancient Buildings. On the advice of the Barnet Record
Society, the two patent sails were not replaced as it was thought they
would cause undue strain on the building. The outbuildings were demolished and Colonel Booth laid out the gardens and had Windmill
House built.

In 1958 the property was purchased by Mr Gordon W. Saunders and,
shortly after his arrival, both sails were blown off. They were later
replaced, together with two new sails, and so for the first time for over
fifty years the mill had her full complement of sails. In January 1974,
during severe gales, one of the stocks broke at the poll end with the result
that the sail crashed to the ground splintering beyond repair.

133

SHIRLEY MILL   NGR TQ355652

This mill, happily integrated in the grounds of John Ruskin Grammar School by the school's architect, was built in 1854 to replace an old post mill destroyed by fire. The post mill was constructed in about 1809 and leased to William Alwen and later, on his death in 1820, to his son, Richard, who later acquired the freehold from Thomas Meager. Richard Alwen died at the age of seventy-five in 1850 and Richard, his son, took over the business. After the destruction of the post mill in October 1854, the present tower mill, which was almost certainly the last large mill to be built in Surrey before steam-driven mills appeared in the 1860s, was built. Who built the mill is unknown, but one report states that Richard Alwen found a 'second-hand' mill at Stratford (presumably the one in East London) and removed the machinery and fitted it into the new brick tower at a cost of £2,000. This could be true, for the machinery found inside the mill is unlike any other found in Surrey. Also, during restoration work carried out by Mr T. R. Nunwick in 1927, the date '1740' was discovered carved on a beam. Up to the death of Richard Alwen, in 1884, the mill was worked for him by three employees: 'Dusty' Robinson, his brother Jack and William Yewens. After 1884 Thomas Dives operated the mill and finally Alfred Rayson who was, according to Kelly's Directory, miller in 1892 and the last one there.

After ceasing work the mill remained empty for many years. One of the sails was struck by lightning and set on fire about 1906 and only the prompt action of the fire brigade saved the mill. Some repairs were undertaken in 1927, but in 1935 during a gale one of the sails was blown off. This was soon repaired together with the replacement of the great spur wheel and stone nuts. The sails were repaired by Thomas Hunt, millwright of Soham, Cambridgeshire, and the replacement of the great spur wheel and stone nuts were undertaken by Lister Brothers of Woolwich.

The mill and the surrounding land was purchased from Mrs Given in 1952 under a compulsory purchase order by the Croydon Corporation. Mrs Given stated that over the years she had spent some £1,400 on the maintenance of the mill. The mill, together with twenty one other buildings in Croydon, was listed as a building of special architectural or historical interest and every effort was made to preserve her. A fund was made available and the machinery was surveyed by J. Anthony Leathart on behalf of the Council for the Preservation of Rural England. Over the years the mill has been maintained in good repair and in the 1960s a new sail and fantail were fitted by R. Thompson & Son of Alford, Lincolnshire, who also inspect the mill from time to time. The ground floor of the mill is used as a games store.

London Borough of Havering
UPMINSTER MILL   NGR TQ556867
In a field, almost in the centre of Upminster, is a fine example of the larger type of smock mill. Standing at the top of a hill and of unusual height, the power from the sails to the three pairs of stones and ancillary equipment must have been considerable. Externally the mill has a gallery around the cap, which is unusual for a smock mill, while the first-floor stage is of exceptional width with an unusual sack-loading device.

On the beam beneath the fantail the date 1799 is carved, but it is now generally accepted that the mill was erected in 1803. The mill was built for James Nokes who, on his death in 1838, left her to his son, Thomas. The estate was heavily mortgaged, so, in 1849, the mill and surrounding property was put up for auction. Eight years later the estate was offered for sale for £1,900, but was finally sold to Thomas Abraham, who had previously been foreman at the mill, for £1,100. The mill remained in the Abraham family for three generations until December 1934, when the mill and surrounding land was sold to Mr W. H. Simmons for £3,400. Mr Simmons' intention was to develop the land leaving the mill intact. In 1937 the mill was acquired by Essex County Council who proposed to demolish the mill and develop the complete site. Public opinion was such, however, that the Hornchurch Urban District Council started a fund for the preservation of the mill in celebration of the Coronation of King George VI.

During the Second World War no work, however, was carried out and her condition decayed. In 1946 a Lincolnshire firm of millwrights, R. Thompson & Son, reported that £400 was needed to preserve her as a landmark. By 1948 a Committee was formed in an attempt to get the mill working again and in 1949 with this in mind the Committee took a lease from the County Council. A fund was started in an attempt to raise the necessary £800 for repairs, but the Committee met with failure. However, although some repairs were undertaken by the County Council during the period 1956–59, the mill remained in a sorry state. Finally, in 1960, the County Council purchased additional land around the mill and the mill house, cottages and outbuildings were demolished at a cost of about £3,650. In the following year another £360 was spent when the site was cleared and grassed. Almost £2,000 was spent in 1962 on extensive repairs including the rebuilding of the stage. With the reorganization of local government, in 1965, the ownership of the windmill passed from Essex County Council to the London Borough of Havering. The Borough Council carried out further repairs in 1967 and in September of that year opened her to the public for the first time, when over two thousand people came.

137

London Borough of Lambeth
BRIXTON MILL   NGR TQ303737
In Blenheim Gardens, just off Brixton Hill, is a tower mill which is the
only remaining windmill of twelve that once stood in the Lambeth area.
The mill was constructed in 1816, and in November of the following year
was leased to John Ashby, a miller of Brixton Hill. On John Ashby's
death, some time between 1841 and 1845, all his property was left to his
eldest son, John, who worked the Lower Mill, Carshalton, on the understanding that the Brixton Hill property be leased or sold to either Aaron
Ashby or his younger brother Joshua. Aaron continued to work the business until 1850 after which no more was heard of him and Joshua became 'master miller'.

During the 1850s the surrounding corn fields were replaced by houses,
and this deprived the mill of sufficient wind power for effective working.
In 1862 the mill ceased work by wind and the business was transferred to
a watermill on the Wandle at Mitcham. The old tower mill was used as a
store and two years later the sails were removed. In August, 1902, the
lease of the watermill at Mitcham expired and the Ashby family decided
to use the Brixton Mill again. A steam engine, later replaced by a gas engine, was installed to drive the stones. In 1912 the Ashby family obtained
the freehold of the land after having leased the property for almost one
hundred years. The owners, at this time, were the Middlesex Hospital,
and the freehold was transferred to Hannah Ashby, Bernard Gideon
Ashby and Joshua John Ashby for the sum of £2,000. The mill continued
to work until 1934, and in May of the following year Joshua Ashby died
at the age of seventy-seven. He was the grandson of the original miller of
the mill, which had been operated by the same family during her entire
working life. On the death of Joshua the mill passed to his housekeeper,
Miss Marshall, under the supervision of a Trust.

In 1934 the Lambeth Borough Council asked the Society for the Protection of Ancient Buildings for a report on the mill and, after inspection
by the Society's Technical Adviser, it was stated that the mill could be
'put in first rate order for the sum of about £25 . . . '. Just before the
Second World War, Lambeth Borough Council and the London County
Council were anxious to purchase the mill and surrounding land, but the
asking price of £9,500 was considered excessive. After the war several attempts were made to purchase the mill and, after the rejection of a proposal to erect flats on the site, the property was finally purchased in 1957 by
the London County Council. In 1960 the outbuildings and mill house
were demolished and the site laid out as an open space. In 1963 R.
Thompson & Son, millwrights of Alford, Lincolnshire, commenced work

on the restoration. Some of the gas-driven machinery was replaced with wind-driven machinery, most of which was brought from the derelict tower mill at Burgh-le-Marsh, while the sails and remaining machinery were newly made.

WIMBLEDON COMMON MILL   NGR TQ230725

The mill on Wimbledon Common was originally built as a hollow post mill and is the only one in England of which any trace is left. The first application to erect a windmill on the site came from a John Watney, in 1799, but permission was refused on the grounds that he failed to produce a plan. In 1816 Charles March, a carpenter from Roehampton, was granted a quarter of an acre of land to build a mill for the benefit of the inhabitants of the manors of Putney and Wimbledon. The hollow post mill and is the only one in England of which any trace is left. The first application to erect a windmill on the site came from a John Watney, in the hollow post, was erected in 1817. The following year a further half acre of land was granted for the erection of a miller's cottage.

The miller in the 1840s was a person called Dann, who combined the duties of miller with that of constable. Kelly's Directories of 1846 and 1855 gives Anthony Holloway as miller, but this may refer to the watermill at South Wimbledon. The mill continued to work until the late 1860s grinding corn supplied from the surrounding districts. After ceasing work the mill remained a landmark, but as the years passed the mill deteriorated and finally an appeal was made by the Conservators of Wimbledon Common to restore her. The mill was rebuilt in 1893 by John Saunderson of Louth, as a composite mill. The original two-storeyed octagonal brick base, which contains the quarters of some of the Common keepers, was retained and the present mill, superficially a replica of her predecessor, was built on top. The cap, which is much smaller than the original, revolves on an inner curb fitted on the top of a conical tower. The tower, which originally contained the millstone and machinery, was covered with zinc. The patent sails were replaced by shorter sails with fixed shutters set close together. Later, in the early 1920s, these sails were replaced and the shutters reduced in number to reduce wind pressure.

The sails continued to turn on occasions until the beginning of the Second World War, after which the sails were allowed once again to turn, but were stopped in 1946 due to wear in the gearing. In 1954 the common's conservators launched another public appeal for £500 to make the mill waterproof and this sum was soon achieved. The work was completed by May 1957, and once again the sails were set in motion. In 1969 the sails and stocks were renewed by Vernon Ely of Wimbledon. Following an inspection in 1975 by the Society for the Protection of Ancient Buildings, when the timbers to the tower were found to be seriously decayed, an appeal was made by conservator Sir Hugh Linstead for £20,000 to prevent the ultimate collapse of the mill.

Over one of the doors of the mill base is a plaque, which records that Lord Baden Powell stayed in the mill house and wrote there part of his *Scouting for Boys*.

141

BIDSTON MILL   NGR SJ287894

The present mill is the last of several which have stood on Bidston Hill over the centuries. It is known that a windmill has been situated here for almost four hundred years, for there is a reference in 1596 to a mill in a lease of Bidston Manor Hall and Park. A mill is also depicted on the Kingston Survey map of 1665.

The present tower mill was built to replace an old post mill destroyed by fire in 1791. The sails of this old post mill got out of control in a severe gale and the friction set the whole structure on fire totally destroying her. This mill was built some forty yards to the north of the present mill and the foundations—two trenches into which the crosstrees were placed—cut in the solid rock can still be seen.

Although in an unrivalled position to command the wind from all directions, the mill must have been difficult to approach for she was described as being in ". . . a very awkward place to get at from the farmer's standpoint . . . the only means of approach were by rocky ascending paths or lanes". The mill's exposed position and the strong winds—gusts up to 100 m.p.h. have been recorded at the nearby observatory—caused the destruction of the mill on two further occasions, once in 1821—when the mill was burnt out—and again in 1839 when there was a similar occurrence.

During the 1840s and up to the late 1850s John Radley was miller followed, for a few years, by James Radley. Morris' Directory of 1864 gives Robert Youde or Youds as miller, but by 1869 William Yods, who was the last miller, had succeeded him. The mill ceased work in about 1875—long before the majority of the mills in the area—slowly falling into disrepair. By the 1890s the mill had lost most of her cap and three of her sails, but in 1894 she was acquired by Mr R. S. Hudson who restored her as a landmark. He took away the remaining sail on the mill and another, just blown down, to have chairs made from them.

Very little more appears to have been undertaken on the mill until the 1920s, when the mill and surrounding land was acquired by the Corporation of Birkenhead and the area was set out as a park. In 1927 a great storm almost destroyed the long-neglected mill. The sails were so decayed that they were beyond repair as was the roof and much of the timbers inside. The remains of the sails were removed and only the tower remained while an appeal was launched for the mill's restoration. Sufficient money had been obtained by the following year and the work, which included the renewal of the cap, much of the interior machinery and four new sails, was undertaken. Since then the mill has formed a focal point of the park being maintained by the Corporation.

143

BERNEY ARMS MILL   NGR TG465049

The finest remaining example of a marsh mill stands at the head of Tile Kiln Reach, on the left bank of the River Yare, near Breydon Water. The High Mill, Berney Arms, with her seven floors, is by far the highest marsh mill in the Suffolk and Norfolk Broads being just over 70 feet high and 28 feet internal diameter at the ground floor. When she was built is unknown for although the earliest date, pencilled in the roof of the cap, is 1870 it is thought to have been built some time earlier by Stolworthy, the Great Yarmouth millwright. Harry Hewitt, the last marshman at the mill, has reported that the mill was working in his father's childhood so it would appear to have been some time before 1840. The mill, built for the Berney family, was originally built for grinding cement clinker, and the stones used for grinding can be seen on the ground floor, although no trace of the driving mechanism can be seen today. The cement was made from the chalky mud dredged from the river bed and also from clinker sent for grinding from Burgh Castle by wherry. The works closed down in 1880 and it is likely that it was at this time that the mill was converted to a drainage mill. This may be why the scoop wheel is located some way away from the mill and not next to or inside the mill as usual.

The mill was used for drainage up until 1948, and in 1951 she was given by the Lower Bure, Halvergate Fleet and Acle Marshes Internal Drainage Board to the Ministry of Works (now the Department of the Environment). The main defect, at this time, was that the trough-shaped track at the top of the tower had split causing the roller bearings to become fixed and preventing the cap revolving. To enable the repairs to be carried out the whole cap, together with the windshaft and sails, was jacked up and five of the eight sections of the track were renewed while a number of the rollers were either reground or renewed. Much of the timbers of the cap were decayed and had to be repaired or replaced, while the fantail and shutters of the sails were overhauled.

In February 1962 a gale damaged the sails. The repairs were undertaken by T. Smithdale & Sons of Acle, Norfolk, the work being commenced in 1965 and completed in July 1967, when the mill was again opened to the public. The repairs were carried out by Cecil Smithdale who, after completing the work, retired and the firm closed down. They were the last firm of millwrights working in Norfolk. The mill was again repaired and overhauled in 1972 and 1973 when the mill was repainted and re-tarred. In 1974 the Department of the Environment arranged a permanent Exhibition of Windmills of Eastern England inside the mill with the text written by Rex Wailes.

145

BILLINGFORD MILL   NGR TM167786

Billingford tower mill, a well-known landmark in the upper part of the Waveney Valley, stands on the site of an old post mill tail-winded in a storm in 1860. She was blown over forwards while the miller, George Goddard, was inside attending the stones, but he was saved from being crushed by the stout main post which held the debris off him, and he escaped with cuts and bruises. However, a man who had gone to the mill to buy some flour was descending the ladder at the rear and fell into the wreckage, being so badly injured that he died.

George Goddard had taken over the old post mill from Clement Bacon about 1857, and continued to work the new tower mill after she was constructed, it is thought, in 1862. The mill was described by Mr C. E. Woodrow, whose father once worked her and in fact worked the mill himself when only twelve years old, as '. . . not large it was one of the prettiest mills ever built. Cleverly constructed by craftsmen it was a joy to behold'. Mr Goddard was succeeded by a succession of millers. In 1872 Henry Pike was miller, and he was followed in 1875 by John Button of Victoria Steam Mills, Diss, who was described as 'corn and coal merchant, steam threshing machine proprietor and sole agent for W. Blackmore & Co.'s patent bolting cloths'. He remained for only a short period, although continuing to work at Diss for many years, for by 1877 Robert Gaze was miller and he was followed by a number of millers—Robert Weavers, John Cross, Richard Wood Crawshay and Walter James Staff—before, in 1924, George Arthur Daines took over the mill. Shortly afterwards he was joined by Mr Chase before finally bringing his son Arthur into the firm. The mill ceased work during the Second World War, but on Arthur Daines' return from the war she was put into working order and the firm carried on. Sometime after he tried, without success, to get help from the County Council for repairs. The mill finally ceased work by wind in 1956, when the stock of the remaining pair of sails split, after which she depended entirely on an engine installed in 1928.

Early in 1959 Mr Daines decided to give up the business because the outbreaks of fowl pest in the district that winter had taken away his trade, and so the last corn mill to operate by wind in Norfolk finally ceased work. Later that year she was acquired by Victor Valiant, who lived nearby the mill, in an attempt to save her, while the Society for the Protection of Ancient Buildings tried to find a miller in order to keep the mill operational. In March 1962, the Society launched an appeal for £1,450 and, with grants of £1,000 each from the Historic Buildings Council and the County Council, restoration work was finally undertaken. The final cost of the work was £3,939 and the mill passed into the auspices of the County Council. Since 1963 the mill has been maintained by the Norfolk Windmills Trust.

147

CLEY MILL NGR TG044441

Probably the most painted and photographed mill in the country, she stands on the old quay, beside the River Glaven, at Cley-next-the-Sea. Cley, once an important sea port, was, in medieval times, centred near the church, but in the seventeenth century reclamation work, undertaken by Sir Henry Calthorpe, finally forced new wharves to be erected near deeper water. With the destruction, by fire, of the old town, new buildings were built around these wharves which now forms the principal part of the village. A windmill was built about this time, but was obviously rebuilt at a later date for she does not appear on William Faden's map of Norfolk of 1787 although she has on the brickwork the date 1713.

During the first half of the nineteenth century the mill was owned by John Farthing and let to John Lee, a merchant. John Lee, a prominent person, not only rented the mill from Mr Farthing but also a granary, coal house, stable and cart shed, while from George Legge he rented two malthouses, a coal house and a house. He also owned seven cottages and one house himself in the town. John Lee died in November 1848, at the age of sixty, and was succeeded, as miller, by Lawrence Randall. Over the years he increased his operations for in 1853 he was described as a 'miller and coal merchant', but by 1873 he was a 'miller, corn, coal and timber merchant, cabinet maker and proprietor of the George and Dragon Inn'. In his late sixties Lawrence Randall retired, although he continued to live at Cley until his death in 1894 when aged eighty-eight. He was followed as miller by Stephen Barnabas Burroughes who remained there, for some twenty-five years, until the end of the century. He, like Randall, developed his business interests becoming a baker, corn, flour, cake, pollard, coal and manure merchant, while also extending his business to Holt and Langham. When he retired the business passed to his sons, but by this time the silting up of the navigable channel, together with the coming of larger ships, made it uneconomical to trade from Cley, although the Burroughes Brothers continued to operate up until the First World War. By 1917 the mill finally ceased to grind, and was purchased in 1920 and converted into a holiday residence.

In 1960 the Pilgrim Trust agreed to subscribe £300 towards the cost of the repairs and the County Council agreed to contribute £500 if the Historic Buildings Council contributed a similar amount. However, in September of that year the Historic Buildings Council reported that they were unable to allocate any money towards the project, but the Pilgrim Trust increased their contribution and the owner undertook to pay the outstanding amount. After this the County Council gave authority to carry out repairs not exceeding £1,300, and in the spring of the following year the work was carried out by R. Thompson & Son, the Alford firm of millwrights.

149

DENVER MILL   NGR TF605013

The mill, a well-known landmark on the edge of the Fens, is the sole survivor of twelve mills which at one time stood within a distance of six miles. A tall rendered-brick tower mill she was constructed, together with the mill cottages, in 1835–36 for John Porter on, or near, the site of an old post mill. He continued as miller until shortly before his death in 1858, at the age of sixty-nine, when he was succeeded by John Gleaves, a local farmer, from Denver Sluice, who in turn was followed by his son, James, in the first half of the 1870s. About ten years later James Gleaves introduced auxiliary steam power, and a new building was built adjacent to the windmill to house the stones and engine. Early photographs of the mill show this building with its chimney shaft.

About 1900 Thomas Edward Harris took over the mill. He came from Southery, a few miles to the south of Denver, where he had assisted first his father, Thomas, and later, after his father's death, his mother, Martha, to run an old post mill. In the 1920s Mr Harris replaced the steam engine with an oil engine. He used this oil engine to grind wheat for flour while the windmill was used to grind animal feed. Mr Harris' son, Thomas Edwin, succeeded as miller at the end of the 1920s, and remained there for over forty years until his death in 1969. On 10th January 1936, Mr Harris entertained his workmen to supper to celebrate the mill's centenary, and in December of the following year he was awarded a certificate, by the Wind and Watermill Section of the Society for the Protection of Ancient Buildings, in recognition of his efforts in maintaining and operating the mill. Although the mill was struck by lightning in July 1939—the damage was slight and confined to one sail—she continued to work by wind until 1941 when the curb, which had been a source of trouble for many years, was again damaged, and with the difficulty in obtaining both labour and materials during the war the mill was forced to close down. The firm continued to operate by the use of the oil engine but the mill was kept in excellent condition.

After the death of Mr Harris in 1969, the mill was left to Mrs O. J. Staines who, in 1971, presented the mill to the Norfolk County Council free, except for legal costs, on condition that the mill was maintained in good condition. Later that year the Council undertook repairs which included the replacement of the curb. In July 1972, shortly after the Council had completed the repairs, one of the sails was torn off in a severe gale damaging the stage as it fell. The opposite sail was subsequently removed leaving one pair. During the winter 1974/75 repairs were started by the millwrights Lennard and Lawn when work to the gallery and cap was undertaken. This was followed by the completion of the sails and fan and by 1978 it is hoped that the mill will be restored to full working order.

GARBOLDISHAM MILL   NGR TM002805

A few hundred yards from the county boundary with Suffolk is Norfolk's sole surviving post mill. The mill was built in the 1770s by James Turner, a farmer of Blo'Norton, who in 1788 built a smock mill nearby. In 1802 both mills were sold to John Button for £795, and some eighteen years later a tower mill was built. All three mills are indicated on the First Ordnance Survey map of 1837, but by 1842, according to the Tithe map, the smock mill had been removed. It was during the Button family's stay that the post mill was modernized and in March 1831, patent sails were fitted. Also during their stay the tower mill was also removed, but when is unknown.

About 1864 the post mill was taken over by William Alfred Lawrence, whose father worked the tower mill at East Harling. During the winter of 1871 William Lawrence caught frost bite while attending to the sails, which resulted, on Christmas morning of that year, in his death, at the age of thirty-six. His wife, Emma, left to run the business engaged John Nunn, from Dickleburgh, to manage both farm and mill. Although he was only twenty-one years old, the business very soon began to prosper until, in 1879, a very severe gale tore off two sails. The sails were repaired and the width increased enabling two pairs of stones to be used and at the same time the mill was extended at the tail to accommodate a dressing machine. Also a steam engine and boiler with an additional pair of stones were added in an outhouse. In June 1892, John Nunn married Mrs Lawrence's younger daughter and soon moved to nearby Grange Farm. After this Mrs Lawrence's son, Fredrick, helped her with the business, but later, when he to married and moved away, a new manager, John Tuck, was engaged. Emma Lawrence retired in 1902 and the lease was taken over by Christopher Pattinson who, with his brother, worked East Harling Windmill. The mill again lost two sails in a storm in 1906, but the lack of trade did not merit the high cost of replacement. The mill continued to grind until 1914 when William Bennett, the miller engaged by Mr Pattinson, suddenly died and so when the lease expired in 1917 the mill was closed down.

The property was then let to Stephen Brock and in 1944, when the Garboldisham Hall Estate was sold, the mill and farm was purchased by his son on his behalf. The mill and adjoining smallholding was again up for sale in June 1970, and in March 1972, Adrian Colman bought the mill together with adjacent land. In October, 1971, emergency repairs were carried out as the mill was in danger of collapse. A grant of £3,050 was obtained from the Historic Buildings Council with an additional grant from Norfolk County Council. With the help of Philip Unwin and some assistance from the millwright Philip Lennard, Mr Colman hopes to restore the mill to full working order.

153

HORSEY MILL   NGR TG457222

The present mill at Horsey was built on the foundations of an older mill in 1912 by Dan England, the famous millwright from Ludham. The older mill, known as Horsey Black Mill because of her black tarred tower, was said to be some two hundred years old. In a gale in March 1895, the old mill was tail-winded and the cap was blown off into the roadway. The top part was rebuilt in 1897 and a new cap fitted, but by 1912 the whole structure was in a dangerous condition and in that year the mill was dismantled by hand, brick by brick, to her foundations. Dan England decided to remove the cap complete, as this was still in excellent condition, and re-use it, but as it was being lifted off the cap circle the brake did not hold, the sails moved and the whole top toppled over smashing to the ground. The new tower was constructed of red brick, made locally at Martham, on the old foundations a few courses of which can still be seen. The vertical shaft was renewed, with Scandinavian Pine imported specially, as were all the floors, but all the machinery and the horizontal pumping shaft are original.

The mill continued to work, alongside an existing steam pump installed in 1900—converted to diesel power in 1939—until July 1943, when during a storm the mill was struck by lightning, splitting the stocks from end to end and putting the mill out of action. With the shortage of timber during and after the war, the stocks remained unrepaired until, in 1956, they became dangerous and were taken down. After 1943 the pumping was carried on solely by a diesel-powered pump and this was converted to electric power in 1957.

In 1948 the National Trust acquired the Horsey Estate from Major Anthony Buxton of Horsey Hall. In 1957 the Society for the Protection of Ancient Buildings launched an appeal for funds to restore the windmill. The mill was not, however, restored until 1962 when a second appeal was launched by Norfolk County Council and, with donations from R. B. Bradbeer Ltd of Lowestoft and others, the necessary £2,750 was raised. The mill was restored to her present condition by Thomas Smithdale & Sons, millwrights of Acle. Taking part in the restoration work was Arthur Dove who had helped in the rebuilding in 1912. He was the last marshman at the mill taking over from his father in October 1918. Since 1962 the National Trust have maintained the mill in excellent condition. In the autumn of 1965 the mill was repainted and the brickwork repointed. Further repairs have been carried out and the mill again repainted in 1972.

155

PASTON MILL   NGR 316358

This mill, situated on Stow Hill close to Mundesley, was generally thought to have been constructed at the end of the eighteenth century. The mill does not, however, appear on William Faden's map of Norfolk of 1787—although a mill is shown a little to the north at Mundesley—or on A. Bryant's map of 1826, which was surveyed between 1824 and 1826. The mill is first indicated on C. & J. Greenwood's map of 1834 and is also on the first Ordnance Survey map of 1838. Also, according to the title deeds, when the mill was conveyed in 1827 there is reference to the mill as being 'lately erected'. Therefore, the mill was probably built between 1824 and 1827. The mill is known, however, to have been built for the Gaze family—a prominent family in the village.

It was in 1827 that James Gaze conveyed the mill to one of his sons, Thomas. In 1836 Thomas Gaze, Junior, was given as miller and, according to the Tithe map of 1841, he owned and occupied the mill, together with the mill house and some twenty-four acres of land. He also owned the cottage at the rear of the premises which was, at this time, occupied by James Newstead, who presumably worked at the mill. Thomas Gaze had the mill until his death in 1872, at the age of seventy, when the property was left to his son, William. In the 1880s he introduced auxiliary steam power to assist in grinding and by the 1890s he was also described as a farmer. The mill remained in his possession until 1906 when, on his death at the age of sixty-four, the mill and mill house was purchased by Mrs Mary Ann Harper. Shortly afterwards the property was leased to a cousin, Thomas Livermore, who carried on the business until 1930.

The property was then purchased by Mr & Mrs Bell and they renovated the miller's house while the mill, like others on the north Norfolk coast, had her machinery removed and was converted into an annexe to the mill house. The mill, although having all machinery removed below the brake wheel, retained her external appearance. In 1938 the property was purchased by Mr D. S. A. McDougall, as a holiday home and the mill was restored by him. The property was, in 1954, put up for sale when Mr McDougall, who had purchased Catfield Hall, required it no longer. The mill was at this time in need of some renovation.

In 1959 the Norfolk County Council first considered the restoration and preservation of windmills in the County and Paston, still being in a reasonable condition, was selected as one of eighteen to be preserved. The work, which included the fitting of four new sails and a fantail, together with repairs to the cap were undertaken by the County Council in 1961.

157

STRACEY ARMS MILL   NGR TG442090

Stracey Arms drainage mill stands by the River Bure, close to the main road between Acle and Great Yarmouth, and derives her name from the Stracey Arms Public House situated a little to the west of the mill. Built on the site of an earlier drainage mill by Robert Barnes, millwright of Great Yarmouth, she is reported to have been built on piles 40 feet long with a pitch pine raft on top. With a tower built in Norfolk red bricks, she has a cast-iron windshaft bearing the date 1880, while much of the other ironwork bears the date 1883. The drive to the turbine engine is unusual for the bottom bevel is iron with wooden teeth.

Both the original and present mill were run for three generations by the Arnup family for over one hundred years from 1831, when the Acle new road was opened up, until the 1940s when Fred Mutton took over as marshman. Fred Mutton—a short, lean, wiry man with a strong 'meysh' accent—came from a family with a long tradition as marshmen, for five generations his family had been marshmen, and one of his ancestors James Mutton, together with William Hewitt & Hindle of Reedham, built many of the drainage mills in the nineteenth century. Fred Mutton before taking over the Stracey Arms Mill operated Manor House Mill, Halvergate, and was succeeded there by his son, Fred, in 1943. During the Second World War Stracey Arms Mill was turned into a fortified post with gun ports formed in the brick sides. The scores of the German air-craft guns could be seen on the brickwork until repair work was under-taken in 1961. The mill finally ceased work, when in full working order, in 1946, when she was replaced by a twenty h.p. electric pump which, like the mill, is fitted with a turbine. After this the shutters from the sails were removed and the mill slowly deteriorated.

It was in 1959 that the Norfolk County Council first considered the whole future of mills in the county, and Stracey Arms Mill was selected as one of eighteen to be preserved by them. At this time only the stocks remained of the sails and the fantail was missing but otherwise the mill was in fair condition. In 1961 restoration work was undertaken by the millwrights, T. Smithdale & Sons of Acle, restoring her to her original condition. Four new sails were fitted together with a fantail, while repair work was carried out to the cap and balcony. The brickwork was repaired and the gun ports were bricked up. The work was financed by the County Council with generous help from the Norfolk and Suffolk Broads Yacht Owner's Association, Messrs R. B. Bradbear Ltd of Lowes-toft, the Society for the Protection of Ancient Buildings, and other donors. In 1965 the mill was presented to the County Council by Lady

Stracey and in the autumn of that year the mill was repainted and the brickwork repointed. Later the mill came into the care of the Norfolk Windmills Trust, and following damage in a gale to the sails in 1972, the Trust set about the task of restoring the mill.

159

SUBSCRIPTION MILL, NORTH LEVERTON   NGR SK775820

Almost overshadowed by a modern power station stands a relic from the past—North Leverton Mill. Built in 1813, the mill was constructed by and for a group of farmers in the parishes of North Leverton, Fenton, Sturton-le-Steeple and Habblesthorpe. A Subscription Mill Company was established which continued to operate until 1956, when a new limited company was formed. The original purpose of the mill was not only to grind corn for the members of the company, but also for other farmers and for the poor.

The first miller was probably a Mr Thorpe and was succeeded, on his death, by his nephew who ran the mill until 1874. George Crooks then took control working the mill for over forty years until his retirement in 1919. Ten years after he came to the mill she was modernized by Thorntons of Retford when the tower was raised, a new cap fitted and patent sails installed. On the retirement of Mr Crooks, George Coarse ran the mill and further extensive repairs were undertaken and a new pair of sails were fitted. Mr Coarse, who was a watermiller by trade, stayed only a few years and was followed by George Foster who continued to work the mill until his death in 1955. He was a millwright by trade and when he took over he put up two sails also repairing the fantail. Over the years he was a valuable asset to the mill undertaking many of the repairs himself. In 1954 he was awarded a certificate from the Society for the Protection of Ancient Buildings for his services to the mill. In 1956 Albert Wilby operated the mill for a short period on a temporary basis and he was followed by Graham Wilson, but, unfortunately, he stayed for less than a year.

A new limited company was formed in March 1956 with a voluntary organization, the 'Friends of the Windmill', formed to raise money. At this time a new engine was installed to increase the scope of the mill and in this year the brickwork under the curb was rebuilt. On the resignation of Mr Wilson, in February 1957, Mr Wilby agreed to resume his duties on a full time basis. In July 1959, one of the sails was struck by lightning and the repairs to this, together with other major restoration work, was estimated to be about £3,000. With a grant and loan from Nottinghamshire County Council and grants from the Ministry of Works, the Council for the Preservation of Rural England, Retford Rural District Council and the Friends of the Windmill the money was raised. All the sails were renewed, a new cast-iron curb was made and a bad crack in the wall, caused by the former curb, was repaired. The work was undertaken, in 1960, by R. Thompson & Son of Alford, Lincolnshire. However, soon afterwards Mr Wilby left and the position of miller was advertised. Finally William Hethershaw,

from a nearby village, undertook the running of the mill. She was again repaired in 1973 after being struck by lightning the previous year. Two new pitch pine sails were fitted, the fantail reboarded and the mill repainted and tarred.

ASHTON MILL, CHAPEL ALLERTON   NGR ST414504

A windmill has stood in the Manor of Allerton for almost five hundred years, for there is a reference to one as early as 1492 while in 1549 an indenture was made for the rebuilding of a windmill. This was probably a post mill which could have occupied the site on which the present mill stands. Built on a mound, she is thought to have been built in the middle of the eighteenth century, and has the name and date 'Paul Wilkins June 22nd 1799' carved on a beam. Paul Wilkins is known to have been at the mill at this time, but she was owned by the Luckins family, for it is said to have been with them for 'over one hundred years', and was worked by a member of that family in the mid-nineteenth century. According to Kelly's Directories subsequent millers were Paul Wilkins (1861–66), Edwin Wilkins (1866–84) and T. Hooper (1884–87).

In 1887 John Stevens acquired the mill and continually improved her. About 1894 he introduced auxiliary steam power, driven from the engine house, situated near the yard gate, to an outside pulley on the mill above the door. Later, following a storm in which the mill was almost out of control, he journeyed to Sussex to see for himself how spring and patent sails operated, with the result that he replaced two of the common sails with spring sails. When Moorlinch Mill was demolished, in about 1900, Mr Stevens brought much of the gearing, fitting it to his own mill. At this time the thatch to the cap was removed and a new cap fitted, of the same shape, covered with corrugated iron. The mill continued to grind until 1927, although for several years only spasmodically for grinding animal feed, and was the last windmill to work in Somerset. Mr Stevens owned the mill until 1938 when she was sold to D. Tucker.

The mill slowly fell into disrepair and despite efforts by Tom Petheram—who worked at the mill from 1888, when ten years old, until about 1897—to restore her she was still in a ruinous condition on his death in 1953. In 1958 the mill was purchased by Mr C. C. Clarke and in 1960, under the direction of Rex Wailes, the mill was completely restored. The stone tower—which was white-washed giving the mill, with her parallel sides, a Mediterranean appearance—was cleaned. The cap was covered with cedar boarding, while four new common sails were made and bolted on to four new laminated stocks. On completion of the work, the Society for the Protection of Ancient Buildings awarded a Windmill Certificate to Mr Clarke in grateful recognition of his public spirited action in repairing the mill. In 1966, Mr Clarke approached the Bristol Museum with the view of them taking over the mill, and on 30th November they agreed to accept the mill together with the field in which she stands. The mill, which at that time needed some initial maintenance, is in the care of the Museum's Department of Technology.

STEMBRIDGE MILL, HIGH HAM   NGR ST433305

This random-coursed blue lias stone mill with her thatched cap—a feature now unique in the country—stands in a charming garden setting at High Ham. It was in 1822 that Robert Tatchell had the present mill built, together with the mill cottage (which like the mill was thatched), to replace an earlier mill situated a few hundred yards to the north-east. The mill was occupied by his son-in-law, John Sherrin, who inherited the mill and mill cottage on his father-in-law's death in 1824. Following his own death the property passed to his three sons, John, Henry and Robert, but only Robert is ever recorded as miller. By 1869 Simon Spearing had succeeded as miller, he was the son of John Spearing, miller of the nearby Heath House Windmill. Simon Spearing's son, William, who was born at High Ham Mill, is reported to have been able to work the mill by the time he was ten. When thirteen years old he caught his hand in the spur wheel at Paradise Watermill, Low Ham, crushing it and having his arm amputated at the elbow. This accident, however, did not stop him continuing in his father's footsteps.

Simon Spearing remained at the mill for over ten years and was followed by Joseph Loader. At the end of the 1880s, when George Parker was renting the property, steam power was introduced for the first time driving one pair of stones. George Parker, a well-known local Methodist preacher, was succeeded by his son, Frank, but he left the mill in 1898 after only one year to take up a position at another mill. It was at about this period that the cap jammed, due to the distortion of the curb, and as the overdriven machinery was now made useless it was subsequently removed. Robert Mead took over the mill from Frank Parker, but he too remained there for only a few years, and it was during his stay that the bakehouse, situated to the south of the mill, was used for the last time by a Mr Duddridge.

Finally Robert Hook, whose brother operated the watermill at Thorney, acquired the windmill, but by this time the grain importing and milling development at Avonmouth was taking its toll on Somerset mills forcing the mill to cease work about 1908.

Eventually, in 1910, Robert Hook sold the mill, together with two cottages and five acres of land, to Dr Hugh H. L. Bellot, M.A., D.C.L., for £500 who, on his death in 1928, left the property to his son, Professor H. Hale Bellot, M.A., LL.D. In 1969, under the will of Professor Bellot, the mill was offered to the National Trust. In 1971 repairs were carried out and these included the renewal of the sails made from Honduras Pine and Douglas Fir. However, by 1974 additional repair work was required, mainly for the renewal to the floors, and an appeal for £1,500 was launched, the work being under the supervision of Derek Ogden.

DALHAM MILL   NGR TL720618

Dalham Mill stands within a few hundred yards from the county boundary with Cambridgeshire. The largest smock mill in the region, she
stands about 50 feet high with five floors, and has a pepper-pot cap with
a gallery around.

The date of the mill's construction is unknown, but was probably at
the end of the eighteenth century, for the mill does not appear on J.
Hodskinson's map of Suffolk of 1783, but is known to have been erected
by 1802, when the following report appears in the Ipswich Journal of
24th December of that year:

> 'On Friday evening last about 6 o'clock, a sudden gust of wind carried
> away four sails belonging to Mr Ruffle's windmill at Dalham, one of which
> was shattered to pieces and some of it thrown 70 yards from the mill; another
> was carried about 40 yards and a third 6 feet into the earth; the fourth sail
> was driven into the mill very near the person who was attending the same,
> but happily neither he nor another man, who was on the stage outside,
> received the least injury.'

William Ruffle remained at the mill, combining the trade of miller
with that of maltster, until his death, at the age of eighty-five in 1855.
The mill was then acquired by George Moore, whose family had for
many years owned and worked the smock mill just across the county
border in the neighbouring village of Ashby. For twenty years George
Moore ran both mills together with his farm and malting business. In
1875 Abraham Simpson was miller, followed, some ten years later, by
Joseph and John Tabraham, who in turn were followed first by Josiah
Tabraham and then John Tabraham and Lewis. By 1904 Elijah Rutter-
ford of Hall Farm had the mill, but by 1908 both were in the possession
of Charles Kerridge. No other miller is given in Kelly's Directories, but
she was still described as working in 1926. However, by 1935 the mill
was in a poor state, the shutters had been removed from the sails and the
fantail had all but disappeared. Sometime afterwards plans were put forward to preserve the mill as a landmark, and by 1938 the mill had been
restored to her original appearance.

After this the mill's condition slowly declined until, in 1972, the mill
was purchased by Frank Farrow who, in his youth, assisted his father at
West Wratting Mill. He was anxious to preserve the mill and to restore
her to full working order. The repair work was estimated at about
£17,000 and in 1974 grants were received from the County Council and
the Historic Buildings Council. In August 1974, a sub-committee of the
County Council decided that the urgent work in repairing the main

structure should be put in hand, subject to the total cost of this work not exceeding £5,000. At the end of November 1974, Mr A. Way, the County Council Planning Officer, was given permission to complete the restoration of the mill.

DRINKSTONE MILL   NGR TL964622

Drinkstone post mill, standing on a grassy hill close to some gravel pits, is a typical West Suffolk post mill. The mill has the date '1689' on one of the massive beams and it is thought that this is the date of erection. The body has unusual framing and has at sometime been turned end to end, the former breast being now the tail. The body, built almost entirely of oak, has been much altered during her life, starting with a square body only 9 feet across and has, at some time, been extended both in the breast and tail with the result that the post is central so the mill is slightly 'head-sick'. The mill retains her two common and two spring sails and is the only corn mill still working with common sails. Formerly a tail pole was used, but later a secondhand fantail and gear was fitted. The attractive flint and brick roundhouse was built about 1830.

In 1775 Samuel Clover received in gift the house, the post mill and a horse-driven mill from his father, Samuel, miller of Nedging Watermill, Suffolk. Samuel Clover, Junior, was born in 1752 and he was, oddly enough, the second Samuel in that same family, for his brother, who was born in 1748, died in infancy. Another brother, Isaac, took over Buxhall Windmill. The property has remained in the Clover family ever since passing from Samuel to John, then Daniel, then his widow, and, about 1900, to Daniel who remained there until his death in 1947. The property is now owned by Wilfred Clover. This old post mill has survived while many have been blown down, burnt down, struck by lightning, pulled down or simply left to rot. She too has had her escapes, for nearly one hundred and fifty years ago when tail-winded in a storm, the gudgeon-pin of the windshaft passed through the roof and the spliced rafters can still be seen. Early in this century the iron poll end at the end of the wooden windshaft worked loose and it was thought that the mill would cease for good. However, special iron castings were made and these were so designed that when in position they gripped the poll end in a vice-like grip, holding the sail rigidly in position.

During the Second World War the present fantail, from the old mill at Thurston, was fitted and the mill continued to work until the last day of February 1949, when in heavy winds the mill was almost tail-winded, ripping out most of the shutters in the sails and shattering the fantail. The mill became derelict and grinding was carried out by the power-driven smock mill nearby. This mill was built on the site of the horse driven mill, the remains of which still exist in the form of the brick-built base. In 1962 Wilfred Clover restored the post mill and with her four sails and two pairs of stones she is, on occasions, once again grinding animal and poultry feed stuffs.

FRAMSDEN MILL NGR TM192598

A very fine, restored, Suffolk post mill stands at Framsden being about 48 feet high and so is the second tallest post mill still standing in the country today. When built, in 1760 for John Flick, she looked very different from her present appearance. At this time there was no brick roundhouse, the sails were common-type and the body of the mill was turned by a tail pole. Inside the mill the wooden windshaft fitted with a compass-type brake wheel drove directly a single pair of stones, while at the tail another pair of stones were driven by a similar type wheel.

In 1836, the mill passed out of the Flick family and was purchased by John Smith, a brickmaker from St Osyth, Essex. He decided to modernize the mill and employed the famous millwrighting and iron founding firm of John Whitmore of Wickham Market—later Whitmore & Binyon. The mill was jacked up 18 feet and the present roundhouse built. New steps were built and a fantail fitted to them to keep the mill facing the wind automatically. The wooden windshaft was replaced by one of cast-iron which carried the four new patent sails. Inside the mill two pairs of underdrift stones—a 4' 0" and a 4' 6" French burr—were fitted side by side in the head of the mill, regulated by centrifugal governors. To accommodate the stones a little pannier was made at the side of the body to gain extra width. After the modernization, in 1843, Smith sold the mill to William Bond, who operated the mill until 1872 when she was sold to Joseph Rivers. He ran the mill for only seven years before selling the business to Edmund Webster (whose name appears in the trade directories as miller some twenty-five years before) and he was followed, a few years later, by Edmund Samuel Webster who continued to run the mill until she finally stopped work in the mid-1930s.

After ceasing work the mill stood derelict until in 1966 a group of volunteers commenced work on the restoration and maintenance. The work was started by small grants made by Lord Tollemache, East Suffolk County Council and the Suffolk Preservation Society for the purchase of materials. Since then the money for materials has been raised by having 'open days' to view the windmill and see Mr Ablett's little museum of country bygones. The body has been weatherproofed and two new double-shuttered patent sails were fitted in 1969. Inside, the original brake wheel, which in 1863 had a wooden cog wheel ring bolted on, was re-cogged in hornbeam, while the cast-iron stone-nuts were re-cogged in apple wood. In 1972 work was commenced on the fantail and ladder.

FRISTON MILL   NGR TM412602

Dominating the quiet Suffolk village of Friston, this post mill has been its central landmark for more than 150 years. The mill, generally regarded as one of the finest ever built, stands just over 50 feet high and was only exceeded in height, by less than 5 feet, by the two tallest post mills ever built those—at Honnington and Thorndon, both in Suffolk. In her heyday the mill ground a ton of grist an hour and three millers and a carter were kept busy.

In 1811 the land on which the mill now stands was purchased by William and Mary Scarlett, who, in the following year, sold it to Joseph Collings when it was described as 'upon which a post windmill hath lately been erected'. One report states that she was moved in 1812 from California, near Woodbridge, by Collins, the Melton millwright. She passed through the hands of several millers until 1837 when she was bought by Joshua Reynolds, a miller from the neighbouring village of Knodishall. She was first worked by Robert Reynolds who, according to the Tithe map of 1845, rented the end cottage next to the mill and also a small yard on the opposite side of the road from Richard William Vyse. In the 1850s Robert Reynolds was succeeded by John and later by Joshua, who had the mill house built in 1872. Joshua Reynolds died in 1883 and the mill was willed to his nephew, Caleb Reynolds Wright, who carried on the business until his death in 1924 when his son, C. Reynolds Wright, purchased her from his executors. In 1943 one pair of sails were removed and, although a replacement was ordered, it was never delivered due to the wartime restrictions on timber. The mill continued to work with two sails until 1956, but carried on for another eight years with the use of a small diesel engine.

In 1965 Mr Wright applied for an order to demolish the mill, but although permission was granted 'in the interest of safety' it was not carried out. In 1968 permission for demolishing the mill was again sort, but this time the County Council Planning Committee recommended that she should be removed to Abbot's Hall Museum of Rural Life of East Anglia, Stowmarket. However, at this time a local fund was commenced to restore the mill, and by 1971 sufficient money had been raised to carry out some of the repairs which at that time was estimated at £3,750. At this the Planning Committee rescinded its recommendations and refused permission for the mill to be demolished. In this year, with the death of Mr Wright at the age of eighty-eight, the mill was purchased by Piers Hartley who undertook some remedial work. In 1974 an estimate was obtained from a millwright for the external repairs and in March of that year an appeal was launched for the necessary £12,000.

GREAT THURLOW MILL   NGR TL672500

A small, black smock mill with white sails and fantail, she stands, outside the village of Great Thurlow, on Dowsetts Hill. At one time it was supposed to be possible to see thirteen mills from her top—three post mills at Hundon, a post and tower mill at Kedington, Ridgewell post mill, one post and two tower mills at Haverhill, Great Bradley tower mill, West Wratting smock mill, Cowlinge smock mill and Little Thurlow smock mill. Of all these only the preserved smock mill at West Wratting and the base of the smock mill at Little Thurlow remain.

The exact date Great Thurlow Mill was built is unknown for she is not indicated on Joseph Hodskinson's map of Suffolk of 1783, but one report states that she originally stood at Slough, Buckinghamshire, and the date of 1807, which was carved on the old door frame, could have been the date of her removal or construction. If she was moved it was certainly rebuilt in the local tradition with vertical boarding similar to the mill at West Wratting before this was restored. Two interesting features in the mill are the very short windshaft and the great spur wheel which is planked in solid.

According to the Tithe map of 1841, the mill, the mill cottage and outbuildings were owned and occupied by Thomas Gardner, who also rented another 364 acres owned by Sir Robert Harland. In White's 1844 Directory of Suffolk, Gardner is described as miller and maltster but, in fact, did not operate the mill himself, but employed, during the 1840s, James Talbot. When Joseph Dearsley took over the mill in about 1845, on the death of Thomas Gardner, James Talbot continued to be employed, but later when Elijah Dearsley became miller, around 1850, Talbot left the mill to take up the trade of baker. Elijah Dearsley continued at the mill for over twenty-five years when he was succeeded by his son, Archibald Robinson. After a few years Gabriel Savage took over, operating there until the turn of the century, and in latter years supplemented his living as a miller with that of farming.

Joseph Collis followed Gabriel Savage as miller. He operated Great Thurlow Mill together with the one at Little Thurlow, which had been worked by his father, John, for some years. Great Thurlow Mill continued to work by wind, supplemented by a portable steam engine from 1908, until 1924 when the sails were removed. The mill continued to grind animal feeds by steam power until 1937, although, as trade declined, Collis too turned his attention to farming.

The mill stood derelict until shortly after the death of Joseph Collis in 1959, at the age of eighty-five, when Ronald A. Vestry of Great

Thurlow Hall, on whose estate the mill stands, decided to restore her.
By 1962 the scheme was completed, with new sails and fantail fitted,
the mill completely re-weatherboarded and the cap rebuilt. In 1974
further restoration work was undertaken and the mill repainted.

175

HERRINGFLEET MILL   NGR TM465974

On the bank of the River Waveney, on Herringfleet Marshes, close to Haddiscoe Cut, is the sole surviving smock drainage mill in working order, not only in the Norfolk and Suffolk Broads but in the whole country. She is typical of the large number that once existed in the Broads before they were replaced by the brick tower mills and finally by the oil engine. The mill was built by Robert Barnes of Great Yarmouth, Norfolk, in 1830, and her survival is due to the fact that she belonged to the Somerleyton Estate, who themselves kept her at work as long as economically possible.

In 1956, when this could no longer be done, East Suffolk County Council agreed in principle to the preservation and, having regard to the national interest of the mill, the Ministry of Works was asked if it was prepared to carry out both the restoration and maintenance. Some £500 was spent on repairs and replacements to ensure that the mill would continue to work for many years to come. The work, which included repairs to the tail pole and scoop wheel and the repainting and tarring of the whole mill, was undertaken by Thomas Smithdale & Sons of Acle, the sole surviving firm of millwrights in the Broads. Half the cost of the repairs were contributed by the Ministry of Works with most of the remainder coming from the County Council, who received a small contribution from the Suffolk Preservation Society and other interested bodies. The ownership of the mill remains with the Somerleyton Estate who receive a nominal rent from the County Council. On 25th July 1958, the mill was finally transferred to the County Council and Mr Charles Howlett, who had worked the mill for forty years, agreed to carry on as caretaker of the mill working her on the days she is open to the public and at other times when working nearby. In 1971 further repairs were undertaken by Neville (Bob) Martin of Beccles, whose family has been linked with millwrights for nearly two hundred years. This work included the renewal of the four common sails which were constructed from plans prepared after a careful study of the original sails had been made. The cost of this work was about £1,000.

Inside the mill a fireplace and rough wooden settle can be seen, for many times the marshman slept in the mill when she was required to run throughout the night. Externally the mill is octagonal, with the tower and boat-shaped cap clad with tarred weatherboards, complete with four common sails, and a braced tail pole with winch for winding the cap. The mill drives a scoop wheel 16 feet in diameter and 9 inches wide, consisting of a central iron frame carrying wooden blades and is enclosed by a semicircular hoodway of boarding.

HOLTON MILL   NGR TM402774

On an eminence in the village of Holton St Peter surrounded by trees is situated one of Suffolk's finest preserved post mills. Built in 1752 by John Swann the mill has remained very much as she was originally built, except for the addition of the roundhouse and fantail, for over two hundred years. The mill was at one time owned by William Fiske and after his death the mill was, in 1761, put up for auction being described as 'a well accustomed windmill'. The mill was purchased by Brame Oxford, but in 1781, on his bankruptcy, she was acquired by James Tillot before passing to John Tillot of Wisset Lodge. The miller in the 1810s was Samuel Banell, followed by William Taylor. On the death of John Tillot, in 1835, the mill was again put up for auction this time being described as a "capital post windmill with brick roundhouse." The mill was purchased by Samuel Wilkinson, a miller from Blythburgh, obtaining a mortgage from Mrs Julia Barmby and later, in 1842, an additional mortgage from James Ecceston and William Gipson. Samuel Wilkinson first leased to William Taylor and, on his death in 1845, to his son, William. In 1851 the mill was sold to John Youngs of Wenhaston, whose son, Edward Gotta, became miller. John Youngs died in 1861 and the mill was sold by his widow, Mary, at auction to Andrew Johnstone of Holton Hall, who two years later sold the entire estate to Thomas Buxton. Edward Youngs remained miller until about 1870 when he became miller at Wenhaston and was succeeded at Holton Mill by William Gibson, the last miller. The mill was again up for sale in 1886 when the mill, together with the mill house, stable and engine shed was let at a yearly rent of £27. 10s. 0d. The mill finally ceased work about 1910.

The mill slowly deteriorated becoming, what one owner described, as an 'expensive weathercock' until she was purchased in 1947 by Colonel T. S. Irwin. Two years later the Holton Mill Preservation Fund Committee was formed and some work was carried out. In the 1960s efforts were made to restore the mill to working order. The East Suffolk County Council, after at first refusing help, was persuaded to take the mill on a long lease and in 1966 restoration work was commenced. The work was carried out by Neville Martin, millwright of Beccles, who had worked on the mill, together with his father Robert Martin, in 1933 and whose grandfather had made the existing fantail. Hopes of restoring the mill to working order were soon dispelled for much of the internal framing was decayed and had to be replaced. Special lightweight hollow stocks were made by Messrs William Brown of Ipswich in order to reduce the weight on the framing. The work was completed in March 1968, at a cost of

about £1,200 of which East Suffolk County Council contributed £540 and the Ministry of Public Works and Buildings £622. The only machinery remaining in the mill are the windshaft and the brake wheel, the remaining parts being removed 'many years ago'.

PAKENHAM MILL   NGR TL931695

Standing near the parish boundary of Pakenham, close to the village of Ixworth, is the finest tower mill in Suffolk. Still at work, grinding animal feed, she is one of the few mills where a complete arrangement of patent sails can be seen in working condition.

The earliest date in the mill is 1835, but the date of erection is thought to be about 1830. She does not appear on Bryant's Suffolk map of 1825 nor on any earlier maps. There is also a reference in Thomas King's diary, a millwright from Thelnetham, that 'sails put up at Mr Heffer's mill at Pakenham' in June 1831. In the same diary is recorded that these sails blew off in a sharp thunderstorm the following year. There is also a report that the gear for the mill came from a mill at the Walsham turning at the east end of Ixworth. This mill is shown on Bryant's map of 1825 but not on the Ixworth Tithe map of 1846. In 1840, according to the Tithe map, the mill was worked by Clement Goodrich and owned by John Aldrich. In 1885 William John Fordham, who had previously worked the old smock mill at Troston, acquired the mill from William Turner. In 1920, when old age compelled Mr Fordham to retire, the mill passed to his son-in-law, Sidney Bryant. At this time the Bryant family lived at Stanton and worked the post mill there, but on taking control of the tower mill they moved to Pakenham. Shortly after taking over the mill a broken stock resulted in the mill being operated on two sails until a sound stock was obtained from Wetherden post mill with the millwrights, Youngs of Diss, undertaking the repairs.

In 1935 a new stock was required and a secondhand stock was purchased from Hingham, in Norfolk, and was fitted by Amos Clarke, millwright of Ipswich, while in 1939 the sheers were renewed from a stock from Ashfield post mill. Again, in 1950, further repairs were undertaken by Amos Clarke to two sails damaged in a gale two years previously.

In 1963, under the Preservation of Ancient Buildings, the then Ministry of Works took charge of the mill and an extensive renovation scheme was put in hand. The work included a new cap, a new stock, two new sails and a new fantail. The total cost of the work was £4,000 being paid jointly by the Ministry of Works and West Suffolk County Council. The mill remained in good repair until 28th June 1971, when she was, for the first time, struck by lightning. The stock was split and the chain at the rear, acting as a conductor, was cut into five pieces. The repairs were not completed until the April of the following year at a cost of nearly £1,000. Also in this parish is a watermill which, up until 1975 was also working commercially.

181

SAXTEAD GREEN MILL   NGR TM253644

Attractively situated, overlooking Saxtead Green is one of the finest examples of an East Suffolk post mill. Rex Wailes writes '. . . The East Suffolk post mills were the finest of their type in the world and Saxtead Green Mill was one of the finest of them.' The earliest known reference to a windmill at Saxtead occurs in the manorial accounts of Framlingham for 1287 which gives an account of the construction of a new mill. As village mills tend to occupy the same position for generations it may be that the present mill stands on this site.

The earliest date relating to the present mill is 1796 when she was worked by Amos Webber, a farmer. He was succeeded by Robert Holmes, for whom the mill house was built in 1810, George William Holmes, William Holmes, Mr Meadows, Frederick Eldred, Alfred Aldred and finally Alfred Stephenson Robert Aldred. In the early days she had four common sails, a wooden windshaft, probably a single pair of stones in the breast driven directly by the brake wheel, and a tailpole at the rear to turn her into the wind. The roundhouse was, at this time, between 8 and 9 feet high at the eaves and the sails almost touched the ground. The mill has been raised on the brickwork three times altogether.

Most of the repair work over the years has been carried out by two firms of millwrights—Whitmore and Binyon in the 1850s and 1890s and Collins of Melton in the 1870s. From 1926 Mr J. Wightman assisted the last owner. The present windshaft, made by Whitmore, is dated 1854 and it is thought that this was the time when the mill was raised for the last time. The mill produced flour until the period of the First World War when, like many other country mills, she was forced to go over entirely to grinding feed stuffs for animals.

In 1947, on the death of Mr A. S. R. Aldred, the mill passed to his son-in-law, Mr S. C. Sullivan, and four years later he placed the mill in the guardianship of the Ministry of Works for preservation under the Ancient Monument Act. Between 1957 and 1960 the mill was extensively repaired being almost completely dismantled and every timber not in perfect condition replaced. A new crowntree was fashioned from the one at Wetheringsett Mill which had recently been dismantled. The work was carried out under the supervision of Jesse Wightman. In 1971 further repairs were carried out by Brian Snowling of Framlingham and John Cross of Barningham, when, under the supervision of Mr Wightman, one of the stocks was replaced and other repairs undertaken. Although in first-class condition the mill is not allowed to grind and the sails are fitted with only enough shutters to allow them to idle in a good breeze.

183

SYLEHAM MILL   NGR TM214777

Near the famous Green and Castle at Wingfield, amidst pleasant
country, is Syleham Mill. This small post mill was apparently erected at
Mill Farm, Wingfield in 1730 where she stood with another post mill.
About 1820 both mills were purchased by Robert Sparkes, a farmer from
Gislingham, and deciding that one mill was taking wind from the other,
he moved one, about 1823, to her present position—a distance of two
miles across fields—where she was, according to the Tithe map of 1839,
owned and occupied by George Dye. On his death in 1847, she was advertised for sale as 'A capital post mill in full trade, driving two pairs of
French stones (one nearly new), two spring sails, two common sails, is re-
markably well winded, and all her gear in most complete order'.

The mill was purchased by John Bokenham, but in the following year
she was re-sold to John Bryant, who had, about 1843, taken over the mill
at Wingfield from James Freeman. John Bryant continued to run both
mills until his death in 1867, at the age of sixty-five, when his widow,
Sarah Ann, continued the business. In about 1874 her two sons, James
and Walter, took over—Walter, the younger son, working the mill at
Wingfield while James ran the one at Syleham. The mill at Wingfield
does not appear to have worked for very long, but James continued at
Syleham until his death, in 1907, when he was succeeded by his own son,
Arthur John. In 1932 a Ruston-Hornsby oil engine was installed in a
nearby outbuilding, by E. H. Knights & Sons of Harleston, to supplement the wind power and an additional pair of stones was fitted in the
roundhouse. In 1936 the mill narrowly escaped destruction when, during
a summer storm, she was struck by lightning while Mr Bryant was working inside.

On the death of Arthur Bryant the mill was left to his daughter who, in
1945, sold her to Jack Penton, whose short stay at the mill was not an un-
eventful one. In the winter 1946–47 she was damaged by gales, and the
inner sail crushed down damaging the roundhouse, while, in July 1947,
the mill was severely damaged when tail-winded by a freak cyclone, with
the result that two of the four patent sails had to be removed. In 1949 she
was acquired by Miss Elizabeth Jillard, a former teacher from London,
who became the only woman miller in the country. She transferred the
breast stones to the roundhouse and concentrated the grinding there,
with the aid of the oil engine. After 1951 the mill ceased to work by wind
power and in 1967 Miss Jillard left when the mill was purchased by Ivor
Wingfield, a farmer at Syleham, who is the grandson of Arthur Bryant
and so the mill returned to the family after a period of twenty-two years.
The repair work was delayed, due to the lack of a millwright to undertake the work, until 1974, when work was commenced on the round-

house. Later, when funds become available, work will be carried out on the body, sails and finally the fantail. In August 1974 a grant of £400 was received from the County Council to assist in the finance of the restoration work.

BUTTRUM'S MILL, WOODBRIDGE   NGR TM264493

This is the only remaining windmill of several that once stood in and around Woodbridge. Built in 1816–17, she is a typical example of the work of the once famous firm of millwrights, Whitmore & Binyon of Wickham Market. Standing 60 feet high the red brick tower has six floors surmounted by a Whitmore and Binyon-type ogee cap, with horizontal boarding and gallery. The mill was worked and owned for many years by Pearce Trott who also owned the mill house, yard and Mill Piece—the land to the south of the mill—amounting in all to one acre. The Trott family were shipowners and mariners and Pearce appears to be the only one to deviate from this, although he was an agent to the Shipwrecked Mariners Society. Upon his death the mill passed to Captain William Trott, shipowner of Quay Lane, and was first leased to William Benns—who later took over the mill in Theatre Street—followed in 1865 by Charles Williams, farmer of Farlingham Hall. He remained for only a few years and in 1869 John Buttrum, a member of a well-known Suffolk milling family, took over the lease of the mill. In 1877, on the death of William Trott, the mill, together with mill house and 'extensive granary', were sold by auction to Mr C. Stevenson of Melton for £1,000. John Buttrum continued as miller until his death in 1884 when his widow, Mary Ann, took over the business. At about this time a portable steam engine was introduced to supplement the wind power, the pulley for which can still be seen on the outside of the tower. Mrs Buttrum was assisted in running the business by her son, George, who finally took over the mill about 1905 continuing to operate her until 11th October 1928, when she finally ceased work. In 1938 the mill was again put up for auction and purchased by C. E. Kenny—a lover of windmills.

After the war there was concern over the future of the mill and finally, in 1950, the Woodbridge Urban District Council launched an appeal for funds to assist in the preservation. Shortly afterwards East Suffolk County Council decided to take over the preservation, negotiating with the owner for the acquisition of an interest in the building by means of a 99-year lease at a nominal rent. In 1952 Thomas Smithdale & Sons of Acle, Norfolk, commenced work. The original estimate for the work was £2,400, but by 1954, when the work was completed, this had risen to nearly £4,000 of which the Pilgrim Trust contributed £800. The mill was re-decorated in 1966, but in December of that year the bolts holding the fan spar in position sheared, with the result that the fantail was badly damaged. In 1969 it was reported that about £500 was to be spent on repairs, but when work was commenced one of the stocks was found to be decayed. This was replaced in January, 1973, with one specially imported from British Honduras, the work being carried out by Cubitt & Gotts of Westerfield, Suffolk.

187

Surrey
OUTWOOD MILL NGR TQ327456

The oldest working post mill in the country stands at Outwood. Built in 1665 by Thomas Budgen, a miller of Nutfield, it is recorded that the builders of the mill watched the great fire of London from the roof. In 1806 the mill came into the possession of the Jupp family and remained in that family until 1962 when Messrs G. and R. Thomas purchased the mill and mill cottage from Stanley Jupp.

In 1929 the Society for the Protection of Ancient Buildings undertook to try to keep the mill in working order and in 1931, when two new sails were required, they decided to replace them and William Jupp, the miller, undertook that he would neither sell nor demolish the mill. The work was executed by Thomas Hunt, millwright of Soham, Cambridgeshire, for the sum of £80. By 1933 the other pair of sails had deteriorated and were replaced by a pair taken from Forncett End Mill, Norfolk. After this many faults developed and the mill was worked only occasionally. Just before the war plans were put forward to repair the mill, but the war intervened and so the mill had to continue work as she was.

The mill stopped altogether in 1949 when the breast beam cracked and the windshaft dropped causing the sails to touch the roundhouse roof. E. Hole & Son of Burgess Hill, Sussex, carried out temporary repairs and later under-took extensive repairs to the mill, completing the work in 1952. The money was obtained from a very substantial grant from the Society for the Protection of Ancient Buildings, the Surrey County Council, and help from the Friendship-in-Repair Fund of America, and the New York Community Trust. The mill continued to work for a short time before she once again had to undergo repairs and shortly after, in 1955, one of the stocks was found defective and a new pair of single-shuttered spring sails were fitted. In January of the following year the stock of the older pair of sails snapped near the poll end. This was the culmination of a series of disasters which had, over a period of five years, amounted to £1,500 for repairs. E. Hole & Son again carried out the work, when a new stock and one new sail was fitted and in October 1958, the mill was once again in working order. The mill is still in working order, but is now used only occasionally for demonstration purposes by the present owners, Raymond and Gerald Thomas.

About 1790 a smock mill was built to supersede the old mill, but the old post mill held her own and when trade declined it was in fact the smock mill which was closed down. The smock mill finally collapsed in November 1960.

189

REIGATE HEATH MILL   NGR TQ234502

The post mill on Reigate Heath was said to be built in 1765, although it was possibly earlier, for a mill is shown on the site on Bowen's map of *circa* 1753 and Rocque's map of Surrey of 1762. In the first half of the nineteenth century the mill was held by Michael Bowyer who also worked, according to the Tithe map of 1845, the Wonham Watermill, one mile to the west. The mill remained in the family until Sarah Bowyer sold the mill to Henry Lainson in 1868, when William Quait was miller. The mill ceased to grind about 1870. In 1880 the brick roundhouse of the disused mill was converted into a chapel of ease to St Mary's Parish Church, Reigate. The chapel, named St Cross Chapel, was opened for service on 14th September 1880, and has continued to this day when services are held at 3 p.m. on the third Sunday of each month between May and October.

The mill was offered for sale in 1891, but it was not until 1906 that the Golf Club purchased the freehold of the piece of land which contained the Golf Club House, the miller's cottage and the mill. The mill was then leased to the church by the club. The repairs to the mill were undertaken by the Golf Club and, in 1926, when a sail broke it was replaced by them. The tail pole was replaced by a dummy fantail, put in the position of the former striking wheel, and the ladder at the rear of the mill was removed.

During the 1930s the mill was kept in reasonable repair, but in 1943 the sails were blown off and these not replaced for over twenty years. In 1949 the mill was again repaired and made watertight. During the next few years a desire was expressed by local people for the mill to return to her original character and so, in 1952, she was inspected by the Society for the Protection of Ancient Buildings. A report was made, but the Golf Club were finding the task of repairing and maintaining the mill too much, and so in August 1962, the Borough of Reigate Town Planning Committee approved the purchase of the windmill. The money was raised and a new set of four sails were fitted, each pair with a span of 65 feet and a width of 8 feet, with the weather increasing from five degrees at the top and thirty degrees at the heel. The repair work was completed by June 1964, the body was tarred, a flight of oak steps was fitted at the rear and a pine tail pole was added. The whole of the work was undertaken by the Council's own workmen.

Inside the mill a considerable amount of machinery is still in position. When working the mill drove two pairs of stones in the breast—a pair of peaks on the left and a pair of French burrs on the right. Both these pairs of stones were underdriven. The mill also had, at one time, a pair of stones in the tail, where the circular housing for the bed stone in the stone bearers can still be seen.

WRAY COMMON MILL, REIGATE   NGR TQ269511

The mill, which is pleasantly situated overlooking the Common, was built in 1824 on land taken from the Common by encroachment. The brick tower, which was formerly whitewashed inside and tarred outside, stands 45 feet high to the curb, tapering from 20 feet diameter at the base to 12 feet diameter at the curb and has an unusual lead covered conical cap. Although she is weatherproof and in good condition internally, the sails and fan staging now show signs of deterioration and in need of some remedial work.

In the early part of the mill's existence Joseph Coulstock worked her. Later, in the 1840s and the early 1850s, Edward Larmer operated the mill renting her from William Lee. Edward Larmer, a successful businessman, not only ran the mill, but also traded as a corn merchant from a shop in Market Square and used a warehouse in Church Street. In 1851, according to the censure of that year, he lived in a house next to his business in Market Square with his wife, five sons, four daughters and three servants. He was succeeded to the shop and warehouse by one of his sons, Arthur. Later the warehouse was converted into the Old Wheel Restaurant.

Edward Larmer was followed about 1855 by Robert Budgen, a member of an old established family in the Reigate and Outwood district. He was followed in the early part of the 1870s by Joseph Henry Cooke who ran the mill, for many years, until his death in the 1890s when his widow took over the mill for a few years. The Cooke family also operated the old post mill at Mugswell Chipstead, the roundhouse of which still stands today being used as a garden store. The Cooke family also traded as bakers and confectioners having a shop—which still exists—in Station Road, Redhill.

The mill finally ceased work about 1895 and was the last of the Reigate windmills to do so. When in working order she had four double-shuttered spring patent sails, but by 1900 the shutters had been removed. In 1928 these sails, which had become dilapidated, were replaced with four new, shutterless, dummy sails fitted under the supervision of Rex Wailes and the whole mill was put in good repair by her owner. The machinery from the wallower downwards has been removed and the floors repaired and largely reboarded. This work was probably carried out by Thomas Hunt, millwright of Soham, Cambridgeshire, whose nameplate can be seen fixed to a joist on the second floor. For many years the mill served to accommodate livestock—calves on the ground floor, hay on the first floor and chickens on the second floor.

In September 1957, an unusual event happened at the mill, for during

that month the mill was visited by Jane Budgen, daughter of Robert Budgen the former miller. Jane had been born at the mill exactly one hundred years before and had returned to the area to visit relatives and her birthplace.

Chailey Mill   NGR TQ387214

Standing beside a large yew tree, said to be the centre of Sussex, is a slender and graceful mill which adds a pleasant touch to the grounds of the Heritage Craft School for Crippled Children. There have been seven mills recorded in Chailey, the earliest of which appears on John Norden's map of Sussex of 1595. The present mill originally stood at Highbrook, near West Hoathly, being built there about 1830 and continuing to work there for some fourteen years until she was purchased by Mr Bollen, a miller from Newhaven. In 1844 Mr Bollen had her dismantled and re-erected on a hill to the west of the old parish church of Newhaven, where she remained for another twenty years.

In 1864 the mill was sold to the Beard family of Chailey, to replace an old post mill which had been destroyed by fire a few years before. The work of dismantling and re-erecting her this time was undertaken by Medhurst, the millwright from Lewes, and was erected on her present site. Frances Codley, who had worked the old post mill under Thomas Comber, was the first miller to operate the smock mill. Later, in the early 1870s, she was worked by Harry Kemp Wallis, and then, for a few years, by George Sparkes. Alfred Lockyer took over in 1876 continuing to work her until 1911 when in his eightieth year. The mill ceased work in that year, but in 1914 a considerable amount of money was spent on putting her back into working order. When, however, new stones were fitted these fell through the decayed floor to the ground since when the mill has remained idle.

The mill was eventually rented, from W. W. Grantham, by the Heritage School, but was later bought by Colonel J. Warren and presented by him to the school. During gales in January 1928 the mill's cap and sails were blown off crashing to the ground. The Governors of the School were anxious to repair the mill for the two-fold purpose of restoring a well-known landmark and to use the mill's rooms in connection with the schools activities. The work was carried out by H. E. Waters of Forest Row, in conjunction with Neve Brothers, millwrights of Heathfield. The machinery was taken out leaving only the brake wheel, windshaft and brake. A new cap was fitted complete with a working fantail, and new sails with fixed shutters were erected. The mill was opened in October 1933, by H.R.H. Princess Alice, Countess of Athlone, but unfortunately, in the autumn of 1935 another storm again ripped off the sails. The remainder of the mill was undamaged and repair work was undertaken by Neve Brothers, under the supervision of Rex Wailes, when shutterless sails were fitted. The mill was again extensively repaired in 1954 by the owners of the school, and is maintained in excellent condition. In recent years the mill has been renamed 'The Founders Mill' and is now used as a scout headquarters.

195

CLAYTON MILLS, JACK AND JILL   NGR TQ304134 and TQ303135
On the brow of the South Downs, a few miles north of Brighton at Clayton, stands two mills preserved as landmarks and known affectionately as 'Jack and Jill'—Jack a brick tower mill and Jill a white painted post mill. Jill, the older of the two, was originally built in 1821 by Mr Ashmar in Dyke Road, Brighton, above the end of the railway tunnel and subsequently moved to Clayton. At first it was attempted to move her with horses, but the spasmodic jerking on the ropes caused them to snap, so after that oxen were employed to complete the job. The precise date of her removal is not known, for although a date of 1850 is mentioned, Figg's map of 1861 shows only one mill and this presumably is Duncton Gate Mill—an earlier post mill built in 1765—which was not demolished until the tower mill was built in 1866. However, Jill was moved before the tower mill was constructed for she was originally re-erected close to Duncton Gate Mill, and afterwards again moved to her present position when the tower mill was built. Both post mills at this time were worked by James Mitchell, a local farmer, who held a copyhold lease, the owner of the land being Colonel Campion of Danny. In 1866 James Mitchell had the tower mill built to replace Duncton Gate Mill which was demolished, except for the roundhouse, while the old brake wheel was incorporated in the new tower mill. Charles Hammond, who took over the lease of the mills about 1875, was an ingenious miller who was always inventing little improvements to his mills, his most notable being his attempt to regulate patent sails with a very large pair of governors and two clutches. On his death his executors sold, by auction, his interest as leaseholder, and it was acquired by William Wood who ran both mills for a few years. Jack ceased working in 1908 followed the next year by Jill. In 1909, during a storm, Jack lost his fantail and two sails, with the other two being subsequently removed. Shortly after this Colonel Campion purchased Mr Wood's interest in the mills, and he later sold them to the Anson family who converted the granary into a house using the tower mill as an annexe.

Later Henry Longhurst, the golfing correspondent of the Sunday Times, purchased the property, and in 1958 handed over the care of Jill to Cuckfield Rural District Council. In 1966 agreement was reached between Mr Longhurst, East Sussex County Council, and Cuckfield Rural District Council under which the two councils took over responsibility for the future maintenance of Jack. In that year some £700 was spent on the repair and renewal of the decayed cap. In 1973 Jack was restored to something like his former glory when Universal Pictures, requiring the mills for a film sequence, spent £3,000 on fitting four new sails. The work was undertaken by Peter Stenning who served his apprenticeship with E. Hole & Son, the engineers and millwrights of Burgess Hill.

197

CROSS-IN-HAND MILL   NGR TQ557217

The mill, situated on rising ground, was the last to work commercially by wind in Sussex, working up until 1969 when damaged in a gale. She was originally built at Mount Ephraim, near Uckfield, in 1806 by Medhurst, the millwright from Lewes, for a Mr William Winton. Eventually she was purchased by William Kenwood, a miller who also owned some watermills in the vicinity. Later, there is reported, that a dispute developed between Mr Kenwood and the local squire who objected, for some reason, to the mill's presence at Mount Ephraim and so in 1854 Mr Kenwood purchased an old post mill at Cross-in-Hand from Mr S. Hallett and in the following year moved his mill from Mount Ephraim to Cross-in-Hand. The mill was re-erected about five hundred yards to the south-west of her present position and is shown there on William Figg's revised map of 1861. She remained there for thirteen years until the surrounding trees grew, cutting off some of the mill's wind, and so the mill was moved to her present position. The work of moving her was undertaken by Medhurst who had possibly moved her from Mount Ephraim. At this time George Kenwood was miller having succeeded his elder brother, William Kenwood, Junior, a few years previously. It was during George's period as miller, about 1874, that the breast and sides of the body of the present mill was clad in iron sheets to protect her from the weather. On George's death, in 1878, the two post mills, together with the dwelling house, two cottages and seventeen acres of meadowland, were advertised to be let, but no one appears to have taken over, for George's widow, Sarah, continued to operate the mill for another ten years.

In 1888 the property passed from the Kenwood family to Newnham and Ashdown. They immediately introduced steam power, working both mills until, finally, in 1905 the old post mill ceased work when one of the stocks broke. She was found to be beyond repair and was demolished leaving only the roundhouse standing. About 1935 the partnership between Newnham and Ashdown ceased and the grinding of animal feed continued under the name of J. B. Newham & Son.

After some time of inactivity the mill was, in 1954, put back into working order by Amos Clarke, millwright of Ipswich, the work being financed through the generosity of Mr R. Hawksley of London. In November 1959, she was struck by lightning, the broken sail being repaired the following year. The mill finally ceased work in June 1969, when a sail was again blown down and, as it fell, it split the other stock. The general condition of the mill was such, that, it was thought to be beyond repair, but in the spring of 1973, following much discussion, the East Sussex County Council agreed that the mill should be repaired and the repair work was put in hand.

199

HALNAKER MILL   NGR SU921097

Halnaker Mill, a landmark for mariners, stands some four hundred feet up on a spur of the South Downs. The exact date of the mill's construction is unknown—one report states about 1740, while another states that she was built in 1790 by Urrey of Chichester—but it is known that a mill has stood here since at least 1540. The tower, which is squat, is constructed of brick and rubble faced with burnt-red Sussex tiles and is rather crude in comparison with later mills.

The mill, owned by the Dukes of Richmond and Gordon, was worked at the beginning of the nineteenth century by Mr Watkins, but he was unable to make a living there and in the 1840s was succeeded by Charles Adames. About 1868 John Watkins, son of the previous Mr Watkins, took the mill over. He was described, some years later, as a grocer, miller and coal merchant and employed, from 1870 until 1882, Mr Hunt to operate the mill. By 1887 John Watkins' son, George Robert, had joined his father and some years later took over the mill himself. The mill finally ceased work at the turn of this century when a storm from the north-east gave her a 'nasty cant' and the expense of repairing her was considered to be too great. Sometime afterwards the original mill house, bakehouse and stables, which were adjacent to the mill, were demolished and the mill became derelict. Later the machinery was removed and the interior filled with chalk in order to strengthen and maintain the structure.

In 1934 the external appearance of the mill was restored as a memorial to the wife of Sir William Bird of Eartham. The work was carried out by Neve Brothers, millwrights of Heathfield, and H. & E. Waters of Forest Row, under the direction of Rex Wailes. The old wooden windshaft was replaced with a cast-iron one from the saw mill at Punnett's Town, a new cap was fitted, together with four common sails. The repairs were carried out, as near as possible, to the 1830 water-colour painting of the mill by William Turner, with a hand-chain winding gear to turn the cap fitted instead of a fantail, which was a later addition. During the Second World War the mill was requisitioned by the army as an observation post, when many of the tiles were damaged by them and, in latter years, by vandals.

In 1955 the mill was again restored, this time by West Sussex County Council at an estimated cost of £1,000. The work was carried out by E. Hole & Son, millwrights of Burgess Hill. Unfortunately the millwright broke his leg and, although work on the new sails had begun, it was not possible to erect them and complete the other work until the following spring.

201

HIGH SALVINGTON MILL   NGR TQ123067

The date when the attractive mill at High Salvington was built is un-known. She does not appear on any of the maps of Sussex during the eighteenth century but has, fixed to the main post, a fire-mark of the Sun Insurance Company dated 1774 and she was thought to have been work-ing for at least fifty years before this date and was, therefore, probably built in the first part of the eighteenth century. It is recorded that she was the first mill to be insured, but this is not so for the Cliffe Mill, Lewes, was insured and destroyed by fire in 1760 and there are earlier records than this. Another fallacy concerning this mill was that the main post was the trunk of a living tree and this too has, of course, since been dis-proved.

According to the Tithe map of 1839, the mill was worked by John Har-wood followed, a few years later, by Daniel Redman. By 1851 T. Hamp-ton was miller and his successor was William Day Beard who remained there until his death in 1862 at the age of forty-two. Charles Davey then became miller, but about 1868 Mrs Emily Beard took over. She was assisted by Henry Ball, a journeyman miller, who became, in 1872, as-sistant miller and finally miller from 1875 to 1880. Who operated the mill after this is unknown, but she may have been worked in conjunction with George Brown, a local baker.

The mill was last worked regularly in 1897, after which she was pur-chased by Colonel T. F. Wisden with the stipulation that everything should be as the last miller left her to enable milling to be resumed should the occasion ever demand it. This eventuality actually came to pass for the mill was used for a short period, during the early part of the First World War, by a Mr Coote. Later the mill was purchased by Captain Douglas Jones and preserved by him. The octagonal roundhouse was modified and opened, during the summer months, as a tea room.

Over the years the mill's condition slowly deteriorated and concern was expressed over her future. In 1959 the mill was purchased from Mrs Douglas Jones by Worthing Corporation at a cost of £2,250, with the proviso that the owner be allowed to retain possession of the buildings, excluding the mill, for her personal residence at a nominal rent. The esti-mated cost of the repairs to the body and sails was then £300. The res-toration work was finally undertaken, in 1961, by E. Hole & Son, millwrights of Burgess Hill. The work was far more extensive than at first envisaged and the mill had to be virtually rebuilt; new windows were made, the body covered with new weatherboarding and four new com-mon sails fitted. The final cost of the restoration work was £4,983 and she is now maintained in excellent condition by Worthing Corporation.

203

HOGG HILL MILL, ICKLESHAM   NGR TQ887161

A black tarred weather-beaten post mill, she stands high on Hogg Hill overlooking the flat coastal land and the English Channel. The oldest mill in the county she originally stood some two miles away in the neighbouring village of Pett to the north of the Church. She is thought to have been built at Pett at the end of the seventeenth century, for she is reported to have stood there for over one hundred years before her removal to Hogg Hill, which occurred sometime between 1785 and 1791. The exact date of her removal is unknown, but she still appeared on a map of Pett of 1785–6 although by January, 1791, she had been moved when William Sargeant of Winchelsea insured his dwelling house for £200 and his windmill 'situated in the parish of Icklesham' for £400.

In 1834 John Sargeant is given as miller, while William Sargeant was stated as 'at Winchelsea', although the Tithe map for Icklesham of 1845 states that the mill and mill house were owned and occupied by William Sargeant. The next miller was Lewis Sargent who remained there for over twenty years, until 1878, when in March of that year the mill was put up for sale by auction at the George Hotel, Rye. According to the trade directories of that year only one miller—a William Draper—was in the village, but it cannot now be ascertained whether he was miller at Hogg Hill or Telegraph Mill, which once stood about a mile to the west of the church. In the 1880s George Thatcher was miller and he was followed by Edward Gardner who originated from Kent. His stay was not altogether a happy one for, in 1889, Isaac Grant was killed when he drove a horse and van too near to the mill and was struck, just above the left eye, by one of the sails. Twenty years later, in 1909, Mr Gardner was declared bankrupt; he was forced to sell the mill, but continued to work her until about 1916 when his sons took over. They traded under the name Gardner Brothers, and continued to work the mill until about 1932 when the decayed breast beam needed strutting, which necessitated the removal of one pair of stones. However, the brothers continued to operate the bakery which was attached to the mill, for many years using flour brought in from the roller mills of the district.

The mill remained derelict, and at one time there was talk of her being demolished, until in 1951 Walter Merricks of Icklesham Manor, on whose estate the mill stands, considered that the mill should be restored. He thought that such a landmark should not disappear especially as she is one of the few mills marked on Admiralty charts.

205

OLDLAND MILL, KEYMER   NGR TQ322163
One of the oldest post mills in the county stands on Lodge Hill, facing the
South Downs, in the Parish of Keymer and a few yards from the boundary with Ditchling. The exact date of her erection is unknown, but according to an old plan of the Oldland Estate a mill stood on this site as
early as 1755. However, although a mill appears on Yeakell & Gardner's
map of Sussex of 1783, Gream's map of 1795 and the first Ordnance
Survey map of 1813 shows no mill, and it is not until Figg's map of 1823
and Greenwood's map of 1823–24 that a mill is again indicated. Never-
theless, the mill was certainly there in 1801 for it is known that Thomas
Turner had the mill in that year. In October 1824, another reference is
made to the mill, when the entire household effects and millers cart
belonging to George Bennett of Oldland Mill, were sold by auction under
a deed of assignment. Mr Bennett was followed by Joseph Beard who
remained there until the 1840s when he was succeeded by Joseph Win-
chester. T. Ashdown took over in the 1860s followed, shortly afterwards,
by J. Asted.

About 1870 James Turner acquired the mill and, a few years later,
introduced a portable steam engine to assist in grinding on calm days,
driving the outside pulley which can still be seen to the front of the mill.
For some years the mill was worked by John White, who served as manager to Mr Turner, until 1898 when Mr White took on the tenancy of the
mill. Later his son-in-law, David Driver, came into the business and,
after the death of Mr White in 1904, assisted Mrs White in running the
mill before finally taking the mill over completely.

The mill was last worked by Mr Driver at the end of the First World
War, but remained in the Turner family until 1927 when Alfred Turner
agreed that the Sussex Archaeological Society should take the mill over.
The ground floor was formed into a museum of old Sussex agricultural
implements, and in order to maintain the mill she was opened to the
public. However, in the winter of 1933/34 severe gales caused damage to
the mill and the local committee decided that it was no longer safe to
admit the public, so cutting off their only source of income. A 'shilling'
fund was opened, and an appeal launched by Mr A. Hill of Ditchling in
an attempt to save this 'well-known landmark'. In 1935 a local builder,
Mr Ferguson, built a housing estate at the foot of the hill in Keymer, and
obtained permission from the Sussex Archaeological Society to repair the
mill sufficiently to make the sails rotate as an added attraction to his site.
He spent some £200 on the repairs, but when the sails began to rotate one
broke off, which was later found to be rotten. The mill was repaired by E.
Hole & Son, the millwrights from Burgess Hill. Since the last war the
mill has been kept in good repair although she has lost one pair of sails.

ARGOS HILL MILL, MAYFIELD   NGR TQ571283

One of the finest post mills in the county she stands in an open field at Argos Hill and is an outstanding landmark. The mill was built some time between 1831 and 1843 for a member of the Weston family—it is believed Aaron. It is known that in 1831 he occupied Merryweather Watermill when this mill, together with Luggers Crouch Windmill occupied by Edward Weston, were put up for sale under the will of John Weston. The new mill at Argos Hill was built on land purchased for that purpose by Edward Weston, but, according to the Tithe map of 1843, the mill was owned and worked by Aaron Weston who also owned the house and adjoining field, while the mill at Lugger Crouch was in the hands of a Mr Packham. The Weston family were evidently well established as millers in the area, for as early as 1584, according to the Parish Register, William Weston occupied Coggins Mill.

Aaron Weston continued at Argos Hill until his death in 1856 when James Weston took over for a few years. In the early 1860s the mill was taken over by Aaron's son, also Aaron, who continued to operate the mill very successfully for nearly thirty years. On his death the property passed to his widow and was let to Raymond Weston, a nephew, who had been working at the mill under Aaron Weston. In 1912 the property left the Weston family when it was sold to Mr G. Wickens, a butcher of Mayfield. Later the property was sold to Mr Lampard of Home Park, Rotherfield who, shortly afterwards, sold it to Mr Hardy, also of Rotherfield. Raymond Weston continued at the mill until about 1916, after which the mill remained idle for some years. Sometime later some £200 was spent on her and was then let, for a few years, to William Richardson until, in 1927, the mill finally ceased operations. The mill was then let to Mr J. J. Fuller, a farmer, but although anxious to find a suitable miller he was unable to find one. In 1929 the fantail, which was mounted on the tail pole, was blown off in a gale and about 1932 the shutters from the sails were removed to reduce damage.

The mill remained in a fair condition and in the 1950s the mill was preserved when the present sweeps and a temporary tail pole were fitted. Since then the mill has been maintained by the former Uckfield Rural District Council, and continued by Wealden District Council with the cost being shared with the East Sussex County Council. Work to the breast beam, side girts and corner posts were carried out in the 1960s. In 1969 a new tail pole was fitted and the fantail restored. The original restoration work was carried out by William Sands & Sons of Heathfield, while the other work has been carried out by E. Hole & Son of Burgess Hill. In the roundhouse is a museum of milling collected by Mr F. Child, its honorary curator.

209

NUTLEY MILL   NGR TQ451291

Standing in the beautiful Ashdown Forest, at Nutley, is an old post mill recently restored to full working order by the Uckfield and District Preservation Society. Not only is she the smallest post mill, but also the only example left of an open trestle mill in the county. According to an old roadman, named Setford, of Danehill, she was removed from Crowborough to her present site by his grandfather. When this happened is not known, but the mill is first indicated on the Ordnance Survey map of 1813, while inside the mill, carved on a beam, the initials 'W.S.', probably a member of the Setford family, and the date 1817. Also, according to the Tithe map of 1840, Henry Setford was owner and miller and he remained there until 1862 when the mill was put up for sale by auction. His successor was William Taylor, described as a miller and grocer, who remained there until the turn of the century when a Mr Rook took possession, continuing there until the mill finally ceased operation in 1908.

Even before the mill had ceased work she had some bad structural defects, and soon afterwards the body was propped up at the front until, in 1929, the new owner, Lady Castle Stewart, strengthened the structure. To prevent total collapse and to take the weight off the rotten trestle, two brick piers with a steel girder were built to support the front, while the rear was supported by four wooden posts. New skeleton sails were fitted, and the complete body clad with an additional layer of weatherboarding giving the body considerable strength. The mill was kept in good repair, at considerable cost to her owner, and has, except for a period during the war, always had a set of sails.

In 1968 a voluntary group investigated the possibility of carrying out some restoration work on the mill. By this time the trestle had decayed to such an extent that it no longer supported the post, while the breast of the mill, the breast beam supporting the windshaft, and sails were so decayed that they could have collapsed at any time, as too were the beams supporting the stones. Later that year the mill was shored up to prevent her total collapse while an agreement was reached between the owner and a group of interested people. An appeal was launched, with the owner being prepared to contribute a pound for each pound raised and this was further increased by a grant of £500 from the East Sussex County Council. In 1969 the rebuilding of the mill began with the body being raised, while new crosstrees and quarterbars were fitted. The existing timbers were re-used wherever possible so that the final restoration should be as near the original state. Finally, on the evening of the 14th October 1971, the body of the mill was turned to the north through 180° to face the wind, while two small temporary sail cloths were fitted and the sails turned for the first time since 1908.

211

POLEGATE MILL   NGR TQ582041

There stands in the centre of a housing estate, in Polegate, a very fine tower mill preserved by the Eastbourne and District Preservation Society. She was built for Joseph Seymour, a farmer, in 1817—a date to be found carved on the brickwork—who later, in 1833, constructed the watermill three hundred yards to the west, known as Lower Mill. Seymour died in 1845, and the windmill became the property of his son, Joseph Seymour, Junior. Later the windmill was in the possession of Matthias Mockett, who was also landlord of the Red Lion, Willingdon, combining these occupations with those of farming and coal merchant. The mill then, in 1891, passed to George Thomas, grandson of Joseph Seymour the original owner. The Thomas family had, since 1840, been running Wannock Watermill which was also originally owned by Joseph Seymour. George Thomas operated both mills until his death in 1915, when both mills were put up for sale, and were finally, in 1918, purchased by Ephraim Ovenden. Ephraim Ovenden, followed by his son, Albert, continued to work the mill by wind until 1943, when the fan staging became decayed. An electric motor continued to power the mill until she finally stopped work in 1965.

In 1952 a proposal was made to preserve the mill as a landmark, but it was not until ten years later that the newly formed Eastbourne and District Preservation Society campaigned for her preservation. At this time permission was being sought for the mill's demolition so that the site could be developed for housing. However, Albert Ovenden agreed to sell the mill to the Society for £1,000 although the value of the site at that time was £2,500. The Society agreed to her purchase and the local authority had a preservation order placed on her. In February 1964 an appeal for £3,500 was launched for the purchase and subsequent renovation of the mill. By April 1965, with the aid of East Sussex County Council, the Historic Buildings Council, the Pilgrim Trust and the Hailsham Rural District Council, sufficient funds had been raised for the purchase. After the property had been transferred work was commenced on her renovation, and in November 1965, E. Hole & Son, the millwrights from Burgess Hill, commenced work with the removal of the existing sails. The work included the renewal of one pair of sails, the repair of the other pair, replacement of the fantail and staging which necessitated the raising of the cap, and the repair and reboarding of the cap. Much work was carried out by a band of volunteers: this included the decoration of the interior walls and the treatment of the woodwork against woodworm. By 1967 the work was complete, and the sails were once again capable of turning. Next to the mill is a small museum containing many items formerly used in running and maintaining the mill.

213

BLACKDOWN MILL, PUNNETT'S TOWN   NGR TQ627208

This smock mill now stands proudly restored, by the present owner William Dallaway, high on a hill overlooking the fields from which she once drew her trade. The Dallaway family have been millers at Punnett's Town since about 1800 and the present mill was brought from Sissinghurst, Kent, by wagon by David Hobden for his father-in-law, Samuel Dallaway, to replace an old post mill struck by lightning and burnt to the ground a few years before. The re-erection was undertaken by Stephen Neve, the Heathfield millwright, with the assistance of Reubin Piper. The mill originally had two spring and two common sails, the latter pair being replaced in the early 1880s with patent sails. At about this time the stage was replaced with a brick base and deck, built around and some feet away from the original structure, giving the mill greater storage space. Samuel Dallaway remained miller until the 1870s when he was succeeded first by Charles, and a few years later by Thomas, who first traded under the name of Thomas Dallaway & Brothers and later, in the 1880s, as Dallaway Brothers. At this time the family also worked the mill at Rockhill, and in the years between 1907 and 1911 their efforts were concentrated there, while the mill at Punnett's Town was run by William Richardson. In 1913 J. Dallaway returned to Punnett's Town running both mills, with the assistance of his sons, for several years. Finally the sons took over the business with Demas Dallaway the last to work her. The mill ceased work, by wind, in 1928 when the curb was damaged causing it and the sails to run out of true. The sails and the fan were removed the following year and in 1934 the cap was removed together with all the machinery.

In 1947 William Dallaway, son of Demas, commenced the enormous task of restoring the mill. She was, at this time, an empty shell used for storing animal feed. A new cap frame was made from trees felled and sawn up by Mr Dallaway, a new cap made and a fan stage constructed. A cast-iron windshaft was salvaged from the demolished smock mill at Staplecross and hoisted into position. An upright shaft was fitted, together with a great spur wheel and stone nuts, while a third pinion was introduced to drive an oat crusher. A fan was made which, through a number of gears, meshed with the original rack which still remained. Finally new sails were made, the last pair being fitted in 1972.

The mill's earlier name was 'Cherry Clack', after the position she once occupied in the cherry orchard in Kent, and frequently appears, thinly disguised, as 'Cherry Black Mill' in Rudyard Kipling's stories of Sussex. Later she was renamed Blackdown Mill and was one of four mills that once stood at Punnett's Town in the nineteenth century—Blackdown Mill, Blackheath Mill, an old post mill and the saw mill which drove a circular saw and was last used in the late 1920s.

ROTTINGDEAN MILL   NGR TQ365025

Sometimes known as Black Mill, this smock mill on Beacon Hill stands within a few yards of the old beacon site. There are reports that the mill was dragged from an inland site by a team of oxen, but there is no real evidence of this, and certainly she was not built to replace any earlier mill for, according to Yeakell and Gardner's Survey of 1783, only one mill stood at Rottingdean at this time—an old post mill to the north of the parish church which was removed or demolished about 1818. It is known that the present mill was erected in 1802, for it is reported in the Sussex Weekly Advertiser of 7th June of that year, that a skeleton of an ancient warrior, was found by workmen digging the foundations for the mill.

The mill was built for Mr T. Beard and when put up for auction in 1806 was described as 'nearly new'. Whether the mill was sold is unknown, but the mill was in the possession of Charles Beard in 1849. The mill probably had, at this time, common sails reefed from the ground as, in 1862, it is reported that a little boy, aged seven, was killed when struck by one of the sails which 'are only three feet from the ground'. Charles Beard died in 1870, and was followed first by George Nicholls and then, in 1877, by Henry Nicholls. It was probably about this time that the patent sails and fantail were fitted.

The mill ceased regular work in 1882, but continued to operate, on occasions, until she finally ceased grinding altogether in 1889. After this it was decided to demolish the mill, but this was delayed and sometime later she was patched up. By 1900 the mill was very dilapidated with much of the weatherboarding stripped from her sides and she remained in this condition until about 1910, when the mill was restored by the Marquess of Abergavenny on whose land she stood. By 1922 the mill was again showing signs of decay, and there was talk of her demolition, but the Reverend Lewis Verey, Vicar of Rottingdean, launched an appeal and sufficient money was raised for the mill's preservation. A 99-year lease was obtained from the Brighton Corporation, who had acquired the surrounding land sometime before, and Mr Verey together with three other local inhabitants were made trustees. In 1935 Sir George Lewis, one of the trustees, informed the Council that he had received an offer to restore the mill. The offer was accepted by the Council and in the following year, under the supervision of Rex Wailes, the work was commenced.

In recent years the mill was been maintained by Rottingdean Preservation Society, who have spent many hundreds of pounds on her upkeep. The mill was seriously damaged in the winter of 1970/71, which threatened her whole structure and an appeal was launched for £4,000 to save the mill from collapse.

217

SHIPLEY MILL

The splendid white mill at Shipley is the finest smock mill in the county, being the only smock mill in complete working order. She was built in 1879 by Grist and Steele, millwrights of Horsham, for a Mr F. Marten at an estimated cost of £800, although the final cost reached £2,500 and incorporated the shafts and machinery from an old mill at Rumboldswyke. The windmill has, during the years, been known by various names—Vincent's Mill, King's Mill, Belloc's Mill, and sometimes Mrs Shipley.

The mill remained in Mr Marten's ownership for only a few years before she was acquired by Mr Vincent who employed a number of millers—Rapley, Ewen, Dawe and Goacher—until in 1895 Ernest Powell took over, remaining there until she ceased to work in 1926. In 1906, King's Land, the land surrounding the house, and the mill was purchased by Hilaire Belloc. The mill, with her three pairs of stones—two Derbyshire peaks and one French burr—remained extremely active up to the end of the First World War, but afterwards, in spite of Mr Powell's efforts, work declined until the mill ceased general work in 1922 although she continued, on occasions, until 1926. In the shed, still attached to the mill, a steam engine was installed which drove, by means of a belt, the machinery inside the mill. After her active days, and up to the beginning of the Second World War, Mr Belloc strived to keep the mill in good repair, but during and after the war, when labour and materials were scarce, the mill became in need of repair. On his death the mill became the property of one of his daughters, Mrs Jebb.

At this time, local people suggested that Mr Belloc's friends should be approached to see if they would subscribe towards a fund to restore the mill and make the mill a local memorial to him. A committee was formed, which included Peter Powell, the son of the last miller. The response to the appeal was outstanding and the work was let to E. Hole & Son, millwrights of Burgess Hill. West Sussex County Council then approached the committee with a proposal to help financially with the repairs if the mill was afterwards opened to the public. The committee agreed to this and work was put in hand, which included the replacement of the stocks, and the repairs to the cant posts, sails, cap frame and weatherboarding. The cost of these repairs was £4,556. When work was completed, a memorial plaque to Mr Belloc was fixed above the entrance, and an opening day was arranged in May 1958. After this the mill was often used by Mr Peter Powell and in fact he ground sixty tons of grain during one winter. Since his death, a few years ago, only a little grinding has

taken place and then only for demonstration purposes. Repair work has been carried out from time to time, as considered necessary, and in 1970 the mill was again completely repaired including the re-roofing of the cap.

WEST BLATCHINGTON MILL   NGR TQ279068

An eminently curious mill exists at West Blatchington, north of Hove, and, although she is now surrounded by houses she is situated in a small preserved area of the old village so the mill now stands, with the church, in an open grassed area reminding people that this was once a small secluded hamlet. At first sight, this hexagonal smock mill appears to be built on top of a barn or, as earlier records show, on top of three barns forming a 'T' with the mill at their intersection. In fact, the mill's body is built on a square tower which goes down to the ground with the barns built around her. The tower part of the mill is most beautifully built of flint and red brick with circular windows. The mill is said to have been built in 1724, but the present structure was erected about 1820— belonging to the Marquess of Abergavenny forming part of the West Blatchington Farm—first appearing on Greenwood's map of Sussex of 1823–24. The mill was primarily used for farm purposes and contained two pairs of unusually small stones driven by underdrift gearing. When not grinding the mill was used to drive farm machinery, such as a threshing machine and chaff-cutters, housed in the barns.

According to the Tithe map of 1838 the farm was run by William Hodson, who was followed by George Hodson, John Brown and finally Richard Brown. During Richard Brown's time at the farm, Mr Strudwick was employed as miller, but, when he reached the age of eighty-five, his employer considered it unsafe for him to be still attending to the sails, and so instructed Mr Whittington to learn the trade. He continued to work the mill for fifteen years until two sails were blown off in 1897.

The mill remained for many years with two sails and fantail, but in December 1934, the fan broke and was afterwards removed. Two years later the barn to the south side was gutted by fire. In April 1937, the mill, with five acres of land, was purchased by Hove Town Council for £3,400 on condition that the mill be preserved. At the request of the Council, Rex Wailes made a preliminary report on the mill's condition, and he drew up a specification for the necessary extensive repairs. The work was undertaken by Neve Brothers of Heathfield, under the direction of Mr Wailes. The work included the fitting of new sails and the covering of the original weatherboarding with unpainted cedar boarding. In the gales of May 1966, one of the sails was damaged, and, on inspection, it was revealed that there was considerable timber decay which necessitated the complete renewal of the sails and stocks. The work was carried out in the summer of that year at a cost of £500. For many years this mill was a landmark on Admiralty charts and like so many windmills near the coast has a tradition of being involved in smuggling.

221

Tyne and Wear
FULWELL MILL   NGR NZ392595

Out of nearly one hundred mills that once existed in the North-east, only four now have any substantial remains and the mill at Fulwell is by far the most complete. She was built in 1821, on the site of an old mill indicated on a map of 1785, by Allison of Whitburn for Matthew Robson Swan, a shipowner, who lived in a house nearby the mill. He owned all the land around, including the quarries from which the limestone used in the mill's construction was quarried. The construction of the mill is unique, for her cylindrical base, which forms a reefing stage, supports the tower of the mill.

It is known that John Fuller was miller in 1834, and by the 1840s she was run by the Dodd family before she was taken over first by D. Coulson and later, in about 1880, by William Moody. The mill was, at that time, still owned by a descendant of the original owner, but a dispute developed and the mill passed to the Church Commissioners. About 1900 a gas engine was installed and the sails subsequently removed. William Moody, and later his son, William, continued to operate the mill, together with a dairy farm, until the end of 1949. By this time the cap had almost collapsed, but the mill remained structurally sound.

In 1951 concern was expressed over the mill's future, which resulted, later that year, in negotiations commencing between the Church Commissioners and Sunderland Corporation, who had expressed their desire to restore her. Finally in the spring of 1955, after negotiations had been completed, restoration work was commenced by R. Thompson & Son of Alford. Their work included the making of a new cap together with the fitting of four new sails. The shutters were not fitted neither was the fantail mechanism, thus preventing excessive maintenance. The gas engine was eventually purchased by Norman Howey, whose father originally installed it, and which was still in use in 1949.

In the early 1970s, following a report by Mr J. K. Major and Dr Stafford Linsley, a scheme was devised to set up a Trust to undertake the complete renovation of the mill and to restore her to full working order. The estimated cost, in 1974, was £8,000, but although Sunderland Corporation agreed in principle to the scheme the economic situation at the time prevented them making any financial commitment. Some voluntary work was carried out in 1974, which included the opening up of the doors and windows—previously blocked up in the restoration work of the 1950s—to provide ventilation. Other work which is hoped to be carried out includes the replacing of the reefing stage with water-proofed reinforced concrete, fitting a new fantail, new shutters to the sails, new doors and windows and replacement of defective timber work internally.

223

CHESTERTON MILL   NGR SP348594

The most unusual windmill in all England is situated on a hill, over-looking the Fosse Way, at Chesterton. The design of this classical stone building has, for a long time, been attributed to the famous seventeenth-century architect, Inigo Jones, on apparently no better evidence than that the style and date were roughly applicable. Now it is generally considered to be the work of Sir Edward Peyto, the then Squire of Chesterton Manor. He was a man of great learning, skilled in mathematics and with a known interest in architecture.

The building was constructed for Sir Edward in 1632—a date found on the mill—and has been suggested, on no real evidence, that she was built as a gazebo or observatory and later converted into a windmill. It is known that a windmill existed in Chesterton in 1636 for, in the estate accounts for that year and the following one, there are references to the supply and repair of the 'saylecloths' and the supply of stone 'used at the windmill'. The reference to *the* windmill indicates that only one existed at this time,but whether this applied to the present mill or to the repair of an earlier mill, known to have existed nearer the village, is uncertain. Further documentary evidence proves that, by 1647, the mill was operating on her present site, Clay Hill. Therefore, it seems likely that the present mill was built as a windmill, possibly to replace the earlier mill, and not later converted into one.

The last millers were the Haynes family. Samuel Haynes, who came from Braunston, Northamptonshire, took possession of the mill about 1880 and with the assistance of his family operated her in conjunction with the nearby watermill. On his death, in 1900, the mills were taken over by William Haynes who, later, also operated the mill at Harbury. Chesterton Windmill finally ceased work in 1910 when the cap jammed and Mr Haynes left, continuing to work at his mill at Harbury, which his family operated until the 1940s.

In 1958 the entire estate, which had been in the Willoughby de Broke family for over four hundred years, was sold and the mill came into the possession of Mr & Mrs G. Tonkins of Wellesbourne. In 1965 an appeal was launched for £3,500 by the Midland Branch of the Society for the Protection of Ancient Buildings for the mill's restoration and the Warwickshire County Council received the mill into their care. The repairs to the fabric were undertaken by E. H. Burgess of Leamington Spa under the direction of the County Architect, while Derek Ogden was employed as millwright. The work was finally completed in 1971 at a cost of over £10,000, with substantial contributions from the County Council and the Department of the Environment. In 1975 the restoration was among the award winners in the Civic Trust's Architectural Heritage Year competition.

225

TYSOE MILL   NGR SP332427

A picturesque old mill, she stands high on Windmill Hill near the boundary of Upper Tysoe and overlooking the fine country house at Compton Wynyates. A squat, primitive eight-sided stone tower mill, which is a striking landmark in an area that has been described as 'the most beautiful corner of the Midlands', she was unique in her winding gear. She had, instead of cogs round the curb, holes into which a pin was placed. On each side, at the rear of the cap, were two horizontal ungeared winches used to wind up a chain attached to the pin and so turn the cap.

The present mill could be on the site of one mentioned in the fourteenth and fifteenth centuries as attached to the main manor. She is of considerable age, and is first indicated on Henry Beighton's map of Warwickshire of 1725 and by 1834 she is referred to as the 'Old Windmill'. The mill was, at about this time, worked by Ann and Benjamin Styles, while a relative of the family, Nicholas, was a baker in the village. Later only Benjamin Styles is given as miller before being succeeded, about 1880, by William Walton. William Walton's successor at the mill, a few years later, was John Walton, who remained there until the turn of the century when the mill finally ceased operations. Throughout her working life the mill operated with common sails and had no auxiliary power to assist in grinding. The mill became derelict, slowly decaying and by 1925 two of her sails had gone as too had her winding mechanism.

In 1951 a windmill lover from Birmingham, anxious to restore the mill so that she could hold her own with any other preserved mill in the country, approached the Marquess of Northampton, in whose family she has always been, for permission to restore her. The Marquess gladly gave his consent for the work to be undertaken and also provided all the necessary timber to enable the work to be carried out. With the assistance of two friends, they undertook the repairs, which included, amongst other work, the fitting of thirty-two cogs to the brake wheel and wallower and a new pair of common sails.

By the 1970s the mill was again in need of repair. Early in 1974 the sails were removed and later work was commenced on the mill's restoration. The extensive repairs included the replacement of defective stonework, the renewal of the cap which was covered with aluminium sheeting, replacement of decayed internal timbers, renewal of windows and doors and the making of four new common sails. The black painted sails were hoisted and fitted in May 1975, with the assistance of eight men. The work, which was undertaken by the Marquess of Northampton, was completed later that year.

Other Preserved or Outstanding Mills

Buckinghamshire

HAWRIDGE (SU948948) A brick tower mill, she was built in 1884 on the site of a smock mill herself built in only 1863. The mill was rebuilt using the existing cap, fantail and machinery, but with new sails. She continued to grind corn until the First World War after which she fell into disrepair and was finally incorporated into a cottage some years later. Within recent years the mill has been completely renovated and four new sails fitted.

NEW BRADWELL (SP831412) A tower mill, she was built of local stone in 1816 by Samuel Holman. She worked for a comparatively short period, for by 1864 the mill appears to have ceased grinding. The mill became derelict and in the 1930s she was described as ' . . . in a bad state within and without, and it would probably be the best thing if the whole of the woodwork were taken away, leaving the brick tower standing.' However, the mill survived until purchased in 1949 by Wolverton Urban District Council, and they, a year later restored her as a landmark. The work was carried out by R. Thompson & Son of Alford, Lincolnshire, and included the fitting of four new sails and a cap. By 1963 Wolverton Urban District Council had spent £2,084 on essential repairs, of which £853 had come from Buckinghamshire County Council in way of a grant and a further £500 had been received from the Pilgrim Trust. In 1968 the Urban District Council announced that a further £4,428 was necessary to repair the mill, but were unable themselves to allocate more than £300 towards the cost. In 1972 the mill was acquired by Milton Keynes Development Corporation from Wolverton Urban District Council for a 'nominal price'. In May 1974, a scheme was announced to restore the mill to full working order at a cost of thirty thousand pounds. Work was finally commenced in October 1974, when R. Thompson & Son removed the cap and remaining sails. A temporary cap was fitted while work was undertaken by voluntary labour on the inside and millwrights constructed four new sails and cap.

QUAINTON, BANNER MILL (SP746202) She is the tallest tower mill in the county being built in 1830 by James Anstiss, in whose family she still remains. When the tower was half built a temporary roof of thatch was put on while the builder went to America and it was not until he returned, some years later, that the mill was finally completed. The mill is at present derelict, but in 1974 plans were put forward by the Friends of the Vale of Aylesbury to restore her to full working order if sufficient support for the scheme could be found.

Cambridgeshire

BURWELL, STEVENS' MILL (TL590665)   A tower mill, she is the sole survivor of four windmills which, at one time, worked in the village. Built some two hundred years ago she has a four-storey tower, built of clunch, rendered and tarred, with patent sails which drove three pairs of stones. The mill was owned for many years by the Stevens' family and was last worked in 1955 by Warren Stevens, who later sold the mill with the surrounding land to a local builder. After the Newmarket Rural District Council's plans to preserve the mill had failed, the Burwell Windmill Trust was formed and an appeal was launched to restore the mill to full working order. In October 1971, a grant from the Ministry of the Environment amounting to £2,850 was obtained on condition that the Trust raised a similar amount. The restoration work is now under way under the direction of C. T. Bourne, John Wisby and John Hardiment.

GREAT GRANSDEN (TL277556)   The twisted body of this old, open trestle post mill stands on a mound outside the village. The exact date of the mill's erection is unknown, but she is probably one of the oldest mills in the country. She last worked about 1890 when William Webb was miller. Later she was purchased by Wallis Mills to ensure her preservation and he made the body waterproof. The common sails have long since disappeared, but the stocks remain, while the body of the mill is supported with the aid of scaffolding.

HISTON (TL442624)   A preserved white-painted smock mill she was at one time owned by Messrs Chivers, the jam manufacturers, and although she had ceased work by 1928 she was preserved by them. She has only her stocks but has a working fantail which has, in recent years, been overhauled by Graham Wilson of Over Mill. The mill was purchased in 1968 by Christopher Woodward, an American from Boston.

SOHAM, DOWNFIELD MILL (TL609717)   The mill was originally built about 1720 as a smock mill, but when the mill had been tail-winded in 1890 she was rebuilt as a tower mill by Hunt's of Soham. The mill, which is octagonal at the base, drove three pairs of stones and was worked up until the mid-1950s by Mr Pollard. The mill has since become derelict and is now in need of much repair work.

SWAFFHAM PRIOR (TL573642)   Built on the site of a post mill, about

1860 by Richard Fyson of Soham, this tower mill was owned for most of her working life by the Foster family. The tower is built of brick and flint and rendered and tarred externally with a typical Cambridgeshire cap. In 1939 the mill was damaged in a storm when the cogs were stripped off the brakewheel and Mr S. T. Foster appealed to the Society for the Protection of Ancient Buildings for money to repair the damage. Further repairs were undertaken to the mill in 1940 to enable the mill to continue to grind until 1950 when the mill ended her working life. Nearby this mill are the remains of a smock mill built in 1875–80 and also owned by the Foster family.

Cheshire
GREAT SAUGHALL, GIBBET MILL (SJ363723)   Built about 1784, this small brick tower mill worked up until 1926 when she lost one of her sails in a storm and a fire broke out within the mill. Although marked on maps as Gibbet Mill, it is thought that this really applied to an old post mill, situated about half a mile away, which was destroyed about 1850 and where a man was gibbeted. The old tower mill remained derelict for many years slowly decaying, until in 1971 she was converted into a residence and four new sails and cap fitted.

Essex
ASHDON (TL595426)   A post mill with a small low roundhouse she bears, carved on a beam, the date 1763, and appears on Chapman & André's map of Essex of 1777. The mill, which drove two pairs of stones, last worked about 1910. In 1974 the present owner, Edmund Vestey, had the mill repaired with the aid of a grant from Essex County Council. The work was undertaken by Bird Brothers, a local building firm. Four new sails were fitted and the weatherboarding renewed and externally renovated.

GREAT BARDFIELD, GIBRALTAR MILL (TL680307)   This famous tower mill was built about 1660, but her early history is now uncertain. What is known is that she was used as a cottage in 1749 and was raised and converted to a windmill in 1751. For over one hundred years the mill was owned and worked by the Smith family. She finally ceased work about 1930 when owned by Thomas Smith, who also worked the watermill to the north of the windmill on the River Pant. The windmill remained derelict until the death of Mr Smith, at the age of ninety-seven, when she was purchased by Mr F. H. Couling. In 1957, under the direction and advice of the Historic Buildings Committee of Essex County Council, Mr Couling converted the mill to form part of a house attached to the mill. Four new sails, a cap and fantail were fitted, but all machinery below the cap was removed and the attractive brickwork was unfortunately rendered. The name of the mill has always been—or at least from 1749—known locally as Gibraltar, but for what reason no-one can tell.

RAMSEY (TM209305)   This Suffolk-type post mill, which stands over-looking the village, was built by Whitmore and Binyon of Wickham Market, Suffolk, in 1842. The mill was owned by the Brookes family for nearly one hundred years, until, on the death of John Brookes in 1937, she was purchased by R. M. Scott, Ltd, the biscuit manufacturers of Ipswich, continuing to grind for them for several years. After this the mill became derelict, but since 1973 remedial work has been undertaken by a few enthusiasts to try to save the mill from collapse.

TERLING (TL765150)   A smock mill, she has the distinction of being the last windmill in Essex to work by wind power. The mill was originally erected at Cressing about 1770, and dismantled and moved piece by piece to her new position, a distance of four miles, about 1830. She was last worked by Herbert Bonner, who took over the mill from Charles Doe about 1900, continuing to work her until his tragic death in 1950 when he became entangled in the machinery receiving fatal injuries. In 1969 the mill was purchased by Mr M. C. Cater, who has slowly been restoring the mill to as near as possible to her original condition.

TIPTREE, MESSING MAYPOLE MILL (TL894167)   A brick-built tower mill, she is reported to have been built in 1769 and bears a number of dates the earliest of which is 1774. The mill, which drove two pairs of stones, had her sails removed in 1927 but the stocks have survived. The mill is privately owned and is in the course of being converted into a dwelling.

Hertfordshire
LITTLE HADHAM (TL438229)   The mill, an octagonal smock mill on a two-storey brick base, is in a very poor condition being devoid of sails and staging, with the framework of her domed cap askew and the weather-boarding in a poor state. Built in 1777, she continued to work by wind until November 1929, when her sails were blown off in a sudden gale and the cap moved. She did, however, continue to work by auxiliary power until 1941.

Kent
CHISLET (TR224679)   One of Kent's oldest smock mills, built in 1765, she still contains much of her original wooden machinery. She was tail-winded in 1916, but continued to operate, with the use of a paraffin en-gine, until about 1922. Shortly before ceasing work the entire body was

231

encased with sheets of corrugated iron—'a veritable blot on the landscape'—but whereas many mills have fallen down the action of cladding her in iron has certainly helped to preserve her.

SANDWICH, WHITE MILL (TR322586)   This preserved smock mill is one of the few mills in Kent where the sails are capable of turning in a wind. Built at least 150 years ago she was acquired, in 1878, by Thomas Stanley whose family worked her until she finally ceased work in 1953. She last worked by wind in 1916 after which oil and finally a diesel engine took over. In 1961 Vincent Pargeter undertook considerable repair work, at first financing the work himself, but later with the assistance of grants from the Society for the Protection of Ancient Buildings, the County Council and Sandwich Borough Council. The mill was acquired in 1968 by the Borough Council which has, with the aid of a local building firm, been carrying out further restoration work.

WILLESBOROUGH (TR032421)   This large smock mill was built in 1869 by John Hill of Ashford to replace another older smock mill. She continued to work by wind until 1938 when the mill changed ownership and an electric motor was used. During the early part of the 1960s attempts were made to restore the mill, but negotiations between the owner, the County Council and Ashford Urban District Council finally broke down and with the increasing cost of the scheme it was abandoned. Although the mill is without sails or fantail the stocks remain and she contains much of her internal machinery. She was purchased in 1969 by Mr T. Robbins, an organ builder, who now uses the mill as a store.

WOODCHURCH (TQ943353)   There were once two smock mills, standing next to each other, in the village. The surviving mill, Lower Mill, was probably built in 1820, the earliest date in the mill, while Upper Mill was built in the mid-eighteenth century and demolished in the 1930s. The last miller was Albert Tanton, who succeeded his father in 1899, and the mill closed down in 1926. Following the death, in 1947, of Sir Sidney Nicholson, who had made plans for her restoration, the mill was bequeathed to the Parish. Some repairs were undertaken in the 1960s and one pair of sails were erected. However, the cost of maintaining the mill proved to great for the Parish Council and in 1972 it was decided to sell the mill on the understanding she was converted into a residence.

Lancashire
LITTLE MARTON (SD349342)   This preserved tower mill was built in 1838 by John Whalley on the site of an earlier mill indicated on William Yate's map of Lancashire of 1786. She continued working up until 1928 after which she was purchased by admirers of Allen Clarke, the Fylde

author, and preserved as a memorial to him. Later the mill was acquired by Blackpool Corporation and maintained by them. In 1968 the mill was extensively repaired by R. Thompson & Son of Alford, Lincolnshire, at a cost of about £3,000. The work included the fitting of four new sails and repairs to the brake wheel and some internal beams. In 1970 the mill was converted into the headquarters for a scout group.

Leicestershire

MORCOTT (SK931002)   A windmill was first mentioned at Morcott in 1489 and the present tower mill was built in 1875 on or near the site of an old post mill. The mill ceased work about 1914 and in 1921 lost her sails, cap and fantail. The mill then became derelict until she was purchased in 1967 by Bernard Wheatcroft, the managing director of a Leicester building firm, who converted her to a dwelling. The work, which took two years, was completed in February 1970, and although the mill has no internal machinery the exterior has been fastidiously and accurately restored. In 1970 the owner received an award from the Countryside Commission.

ULLESTHORPE (SP506877)   This tower mill, with her seven floors, was built in 1800 and continued to work until the turn of the century when she was struck by lightning and the sails set on fire. After this she became derelict until in the 1970s she was purchased by Duncan Goodacre of Ashby Parva. In 1973 Mr Goodacre engaged a local builder, Wilfred Smith, to undertake some remedial work to secure her against the weather, but it is Mr Goodacre's intention to restore her to full working order.

WHISSENDINE (SK823142)   This fine tall tower mill is virtually complete internally but has no sails. Much restoration work has been undertaken by Nigel Moon of Leicester, who has over the years been engaged in cleaning up, painting, greasing the ironwork, making new stone casings and hoppers and other work. The mill was also one of the first to be given an aluminium cap. In February 1972, the mill had a Preservation Order placed on her as a building of special architectural or historic interest. Miss Plydell-Bouverie, who owned the mill for many years, and did much to preserve her died in 1972.

WYMONDHAM (SK850193)   Built in 1814 this semi-derelict tower mill is one of the important windmills in the county. She is virtually complete, except for her six sails and fantail, and at the side of the mill there still remains the steam-engine house which drove the pulley projecting from the side of the mill. In February 1975, an attempt was made by Mr M. Powderly, Melton Borough Council planning officer, to restore the mill, but insufficient support was forthcoming and in May of that year the mill was put up for sale for £5,000.

London
KESTON (TQ415640)   A post mill built in 1716—a date carved on the main post—she is preserved by her owner and is complete except for her sails of which only the stocks remain. The mill is thought to have ceased operations in 1878 when damaged in a gale. The mill was extensively repaired in 1914, with financial assistance from local inhabitants, under the supervision of the Society for the Protection of Ancient Buildings. In 1935 further work was undertaken, but the Society for the Protection of Ancient Buildings recommended that new sails should not be fitted thus preventing strain on the old structure. The mill has been kept in good repair by the present owner Mr R. Fells, whose father owned the mill and mill house before him.

Merseyside
GAYTON (SJ277812)   This two-storey tower mill, built of local red sandstone, is the oldest surviving and the most interesting of the remaining windmills in the Wirral. Now derelict, she has not worked since about 1875, and although her roof boarding has long since disappeared, she contains much of her old wooden machinery including a timber windshaft morticed to receive the stocks. In 1969 an attempt was made by the Gayton Common and District Residents' Association to ensure her future, but nothing, as yet, has been achieved and she remains a ruin half-covered with ivy.

GREAT CROSBY (SD329003)   A brick tower mill, she was the last windmill to work in the North-west being built for William Blundell by William Murray, an engineer from Chester-le-Street, Durham, in 1813–14. By 1859 auxiliary steam power had been introduced and by the end of the century wind power had been replaced completely and the sails and fantail were removed. At this time George Waterhouse became miller and the mill was purchased by Joseph Colton, who replaced the steam engine with a gas one. At this time the sails, cap, fantail and balcony were replaced, although the mill never again worked by wind. The mill was worked by the Waterhouse family up to 1972—the gas engine being replaced, in 1940, by electric power—when Mr H. Waterhouse retired. After much discussion on the mill's future, permission was finally given by Crosby Borough Council to convert her into a dwelling.

Norfolk
BURNHAM OVERY (TF838438)   This large brick tower mill was built in 1816 by John Savory to supplement his watermill situated at the foot of

the hill. She remained in the Savory family until about 1900 when both mills were occupied first by Sidney F. Dewing and finally by Sidney Everitt. The windmill ceased work in 1914, when she was tail-winded, and some time later all her machinery was torn out and sold for scrap, although she retained her sails and most of her fantail. In 1926 the mill was purchased by Mr H. C. Hughes, who converted her into a residence. In 1956 Mr Hughes was anxious to present the mill to the National Trust, but before they would take her over they required the mill to be put in good condition. Although receiving no financial help from Norfolk County Council, he undertook the repairs engaging R. Thompson & Son of Alford, Lincolnshire, and they fitted new sails, fantail, cap and gallery. He also had to provide an endorsement of £1,300 for the mill's future preservation. Finally, in 1958 the National Trust accepted the mill, and now both the windmill and the watermill are National Trust properties.

CASTON (TL951982)   This black-tarred tower mill was built in 1864 for Edward Wyer, a local baker, who continued to work her until his death in 1897, at the age of seventy-six, when his son, James, took over. He was followed about 1910 by Benjamin Knott, a distant relation of Edward Wyer, and later went into partnership with his son, Edward. The mill continued to work, with the assistance of steam power introduced in the late 1920s, until 1940. The mill became derelict until in June 1970, she was purchased by John Lawn, who is slowly restoring her to full working order.

ST OLAVES (TM450998)   Built in 1910 by Dan England, the Ludham millwright, she is the only surviving smock drainage mill with patent sails and fantail. She became redundant in 1957, when she was replaced by an electric pump. In 1959 the Somerleyton Estate gave the mill, in trust, to a committee formed to preserve her. She was severely damaged by gales in 1960, after which an appeal was launched and two new sails fitted. In 1970 the Suffolk Preservation Society took over responsibility for the mill, and East Suffolk County Council agreed to contribute £100 towards the cost of repair. In 1972 a grant was obtained from the Society for the Protection of Ancient Buildings, but the local government reorganization delayed restoration work and the mill was transferred to Norfolk. Work was finally commenced in the early part of 1975, being undertaken by Philip Lennard, with a further grant from Norfolk County Council.

STALHAM, HUNSETT MILL (TG363240)   This preserved drainage mill stands on the River Ant and bears a date of 1698. The mill has, however, obviously been rebuilt on the site of an old mill, probably at about the time when the land was enclosed in 1807. The estate, on which the mill stood, at one time belonged to Mr H. G. Sands, and the mill was sold with the marshman's cottage to Mr Edgcumbe, who subsequently removed all the wooden gearing. The present excellent condition of the mill is due to the work carried out by the Norfolk County Council.

SUTTON (TG396239)   Sutton mill is the largest tower mill still standing in the country being ten storeys and nearly eighty feet high. She was built in 1857 on the site of a smock mill—herself built in 1787 and which was destroyed by fire—for Thomas Worts, a farmer, maltster, corn merchant and brick and tile maker, whose family were one of the principle land-owners in the area. She has always remained in the Worts family passing from Thomas to his son, Frank. The mill, which drove four pairs of stones, finally ceased work in 1941, when she was struck by lightning, after which she became derelict. In 1959 she was included on the Norfolk County Council's list for preservation, but, apart from some remedial work undertaken to the cap, no work has yet been carried out.

THURNE (TG401159)   Standing at the junction of the River Thurne and Thurne Staithe, this small preserved drainage mill was built in 1820, on a piece of land called 'Mill Hill', for the Commissioners of Drainage and subsequently 'hained' or raised by Dan England, the Ludham mill-wright. In 1949 she was purchased by Mr R. D. Morse, who was assisted in the restoration work by Albert England, a nephew of the famous mill-wright. In 1962 the mill was again repaired by Thomas Smithdale & Son of Acle, when four new sails were fitted under the County Council's scheme to repair mills.

Suffolk
BUXHALL (TL996577)   A large brick tower mill, she was built in 1860 to replace a smock mill, that had been built in 1815 on the site of another mill, that had been burnt to the ground the previous year. The present mill was built by William Bear of Sudbury, a millwright and machine maker, from materials from the smock mill, on a labour and material basis, for the total cost of £353. 6s. 9d. for materials and £152. 18s. 6d. for labour. The mill was built for the Clover family, who had acquired the site in 1815, and had the previous mill built. The mill continued to work by wind until 1929 when the sails were damaged in a gale and were removed. Grinding continued by the use of an oil engine and although now no longer working she still contains most of her machinery and the oil engine.

STANTON (TL972733)   Although now semi-derelict, this small typical West Suffolk post mill still has the remains of two patent sails and part of

236

the fantail assembly. She was built in 1791 and was worked for many years by the Bryant family, but about 1920, when Sydney Bryant acquired Pakenham tower mill on the death of his father-in-law, he abandoned Stanton Mill. The mill was left until the 1930s and in 1938 an appeal was made by the Society for the Protection of Ancient Buildings for £160 for the mill's preservation. The work included a fan, four new sails and one stock and also repairs to the carcase and roundhouse.

THORPENESS (TM467598)   This post mill was originally erected as a corn mill, at Aldringham, in 1803. In 1924 the mill was moved to her present position, the milling machinery removed and she was adapted to pump water to the nearby 'House in the Clouds' Water Tower. The work was carried out by Amos Clarke, millwright of Ipswich, and the work included the building of the square roundhouse. The mill, which is preserved, has not worked since the Second World War. In 1972 she was badly damaged in a gale, when the fantail collapsed and the sails damaged.

Surrey
LOWFIELD HEATH (TQ270399)   The exact date of this eighteenth-century mill is unknown. She ceased work by wind about 1880, but continued into the late 1890s by the use of a portable steam engine. The mill remained derelict until shortly before the Second World War when four shorter dummy sails were fitted and the weatherboarding repaired. After this the mill deteriorated, with much of the machinery being removed, until 1971 when restoration to the body was undertaken by E. Hole & Son of Burgess Hill, The work was carried out under the auspices of the Society for the Protection of Ancient Buildings with grants from the Surrey County Council and the Dorking Urban District Council.

Sussex
EARNLEY (SZ817984)   The exact date of this smock mill's erection is unknown, but she contains some machinery which is thought to be of eighteenth-century date. A stone with the inscription 'F.B. 1827' is in the brickwork and is believed to be the date when the mill was raised. The mill was owned and worked by the Stevens family for over one hundred years, and finally ceased work at the end of the Second World War. In 1960 Mr C. N. Darby, the owner, commenced work on the mill's restoration with the help of E. Hole & Son, millwrights of Burgess Hill. It was at this time that the common sails which were in a dangerous condition, were removed. In 1975 Mr Darby undertook further repairs and renovations.

PATCHAM (TQ292086)   This tower mill was built in 1884–85 and was the last windmill to be built in the county. The tower was built by Henry Hubbard of Preston and the millwrighting was undertaken by John Holloway, millwright of Shoreham. The brick tower cost £300 and the complete mill a total of £1,400. She was built for Joseph Harris and has a cement-rendered tower with very little batter, with an unusual-shaped cap which was originally covered with zinc. Some three years after the mill was built the tower developed a crack and an iron band was fitted. The mill ceased work about 1924 when in the occupation of Mrs Harriett Harris, who had taken over the mill on the death of her husband, Joseph, in 1903. At this time the mill was in a poor condition, but in 1925 the mill was put into 'first-rate working order' by Mr Chater-Lea. During the Second World War and up to 1950 the mill was used by the Home Guard. The mill was last repaired in June 1972, by Vincent Pargeter and Philip Lennard when new stocks, sails and fantail were fitted. At this time the body received a coat of white paint and the cap was covered with Ruberoid felt tiles. A substantial contribution towards the cost was made by Brighton Corporation.

SELSEY, MEDMERRY MILL (SZ844935)   This brick built tower mill was restored by her owners, The White Horse Caravan Company Ltd, in 1960–61. There has been a mill here for hundreds of years, the original one being a tide mill. However, on the encroachment of the sea during the middle of the eighteenth century the tide mill was substituted by a windmill. After falling into disuse towards the end of the nineteenth century, the mill was dismantled leaving only the tower to which was fitted a new windshaft, with patent sails, cap, fantail and inside an oat roller. The mill finally ceased work about 1920 after which she became derelict. The mill is now used as an office for the caravan site.

STONE CROSS (TQ620043)   Built in 1876–77 by F. Neve & Son, millwrights of Heathfield, she is a cement-rendered brick tower mill with unusual round windows with spoke-like divisions. She lost two sails in the 1920s but continued to operate for many years with two. The mill still has two sails and is being preserved by her owner, a local shopkeeper, who has over the past few years carried out the work single-handed.

WINCHELSEA, ST LEONARD'S MILL (TQ902176)   One of the oldest post mills in the county she is said to have been built in 1760 and moved to her present position, a distance of two hundred yards, about 1810. The mill was worked for nearly one hundred years by the Sharpe family and ceased work about 1904. The mill was restored in 1935–36 to something like her former condition. Repair work has been carried out from time to time, but in 1954 the Mayor of Winchelsea, Mr Freeman, offered the mill plus £100 for anyone willing to accept the responsibility for the mill's up-keep. At this time £500 was needed for the mill's repair.

Warwickshire

BALSALL COMMON (SP249757)   This brick tower mill was built in 1826 on the site of an old post mill. She was worked by the Hammond family for well over one hundred years and continued to work by wind until 1932 when the sails were removed, but she continued to grind with the aid of an engine until 1948. The mill was later purchased by Mr G. Field and in 1973 restoration on the mill was commenced by Derek Ogden, millwright of Great Alne, Warwickshire. A grant of £3,800 was made by the Historic Buildings Council to meet half the estimated cost of the work, provided the mill was opened to the public at least one day a week. The work, which included a new cap and four new sails, was completed in April 1975.

NAPTON (SP458613)   There has been a mill at Napton since before 1348 when Adam de Napton and his wife, Ellen, settled two mills on themselves. The predecessor of the present mill on Butt Hill can trace as far back as 1543 and the present brick tower mill was probably built at the end of the eighteenth century. The mill continued to work until about 1900. In 1924 some of the millstones were removed and taken to Har-bury Mill. The mill slowly deteriorated, although she retained two of her sails into the 1970s and was used for many years as a store. In the late 1960s there was concern that the mill might collapse due to the nearby clay works and there was a local petition for the mill's preservation. In December 1970, it was announced that Mr L. Sheasby, the owner, would undertake the restoration although he was unable to obtain a grant from Warwickshire County Council. The work was undertaken in 1973 at a cost of between £3,000 and £4,000. The work included a new cap, covered with aluminium, and four new sails.

Wiltshire

WILTON (SU276616)   A landmark in the area, the mill stands on a chalk ridge about half a mile outside the village. A five storey tower mill she was built in 1821 as a result of the destruction of Great Bedwyn Town Watermill, and the subsequent loss of water on the construction of the Kennett & Avon Canal and the nearby Crofton Pumping Station in 1810. George Barnes was miller until 1867 when his son, John, took over. Subsequent millers were T. Griffiths, J. Wells and finally the Potter family, who continued to work the mill until about 1920. The estate was sold in 1929 and the sails were removed in the early 1930s. The mill became derelict until in 1971 the mill was purchased by Wilt-shire County Council and leased to the Wiltshire Historic Buildings

Trust, who sponsored the mill's restoration to complete working order. £14,000 was estimated as being required to restore the mill and contributions were received from the Wiltshire County Council, Marlborough and Ramsbury Rural District Council, the Historic Buildings Council and the Wiltshire Historic Buildings Trust. Work was commenced in 1972, with the repairs to the structure being undertaken by the building firm Messrs Rendalls—these included the renewal of the floors, doors and windows—while Derek Ogden was engaged as millwright. At this time it was hoped that the work would be completed by 1973, but work was delayed and the cost rose to £19,000. Work was held up for over a year, but in the spring of 1975 work was again commenced when Messrs Rendalls constructed the stage. Mr Ogden, who was at this time leaving the country to construct a windmill at Yorktown, U.S.A., was replaced by a Suffolk firm of millwrights. The cap and fantail, made by Mr Ogden but not fitted, was installed by the new millwrights and they also restored the machinery within the mill, and made and fitted the new sails. The final cost of the work was in the region of £25,000.

Glossary

Air Brakes: Longitudinal shutters used on occasions in conjunction with the ordinary shutters to reduce the speed of the sail in strong winds.

Air Poles: Diagonal control rods connecting the shutter bars to the striking gear on roller reefing sails.

Annular Sail: Circular sail with single row of shutters.

Angle of Weather: The twist in a sail resembling that of a propeller to catch the wind and give driving power.

Backstays: Timber struts at the back of the sail which provides support for the sail bars and maintains the angle of weather.

Balance Weights: Discs of lead or iron carried on a threaded screw and inserted in the runner stone to achieve perfect balance.

Bay: The space between the sail bars of shuttered sails.

Bed Stone: The lower stationary stone in a pair of millstones.

Bell Alarm: A warning bell which rings to warn the miller that the hopper is empty of grain.

Bill: A hard steel double-ended wedge cutting tool held in a wooden handle or thrift used for dressing millstones.

Bins: For storing of grain, usually on the top floor of the mill.

Blue Stone: See Cullin Stone.

Body: The upper, timber, revolving part of a post mill which contains the machinery.

Bollard: The horizontal barrel of a sack hoist.

Bolter: An early device for dressing flour employing a cylindrical frame covered with cloth.

Brake: The band brake of wood or iron around the brake wheel working on its outer rim and controlled by a brake lever.

Brake Wheel: The largest wheel in the mill fixed on the windshaft and driving the wallower.

Bray or Brayer: Intermediate beam or lever used for adjusting the gap between the millstones supporting the free end of the bridge tree.

Breast Beam: The main horizontal beam supporting the neck of the windshaft.

Breast of a Mill: The front of a post mill between the main post and the sails.

Breast of a Millstone: The middle third of the grinding face.

Bridge: The curved bar across the eye of the runner stone enabling it to be fixed to the stone spindle.

Bridge Tree: A beam supporting the footstep bearing of the stone spindle.

Bridging Box: The bearing box on the bridge tree supporting the stone spindle complete with screws for lateral adjustment.

Bridle Irons: The couplings used to fasten a sail back to the arm of an iron cross.

Buck: An East Anglian term for the body of a post mill.

Burr Stone: See French Stone.

Canister: See Poll End.

Cant Post: The corner post of a smock mill.

Canvas: The cloths that are spread on a common sail.

Cap: The revolving top of a tower or smock mill.

Cap Circle: The circular, timber sub-frame from which the rafters rise on some caps.

Cap Frame: The horizontal timber frame which forms the base of the cap.

Cap Piece: The rear tie beam of the sheers.

Cap Spars or Ribs: The rafters of the cap.

Casing: See Vat.

Centre Beam: The main central beam of the cap frame.

Chain Posts: The posts used to fasten the ends of the anchor chains used in winding a mill with a tail pole.

Chain Purchase Wheel: A Suffolk term for a Y-wheel.

Clam: An iron grip with ring for insertion into the side of a millstone for lifting the stone.

Clamps: The wooden members bolted to both sides of the stocks and locking the sail units in the poll end.

Clapper: A device to control the flow of grain to the stones from the shoe.

Clasp Arm Wheel: A timber wheel built up on a cruciform frame consisting of two pairs of parallel spokes enclosing the axle.

Cloth Sails: See Common Sails.

Cloths: See Canvas.

Cock Head: The rounded top end of the stone spindle.

Collar: The bearing round the main post under the body of the post mill.

Common Sails: Sails which are spread with canvas.

Compass Arm Wheel: A wooden gear wheel with the arms mounted through the shaft.

Composite Mill: A post mill body supported on a short tower.

Composition Stones: Stones manufactured from cement and carborundum or emery.

Cracking: The process of cutting fine grooves in the surface of the lands of the millstone.

Crook String: A cord to control the angle of the shoe feeding grain to the stones.

Cross: The multi-armed iron casting fixed to the end of a windshaft to carry sails which have no stocks.

Crosstrees: The two main horizontal beams crossing one another at the middle and forming the framework of the post mill.

Crowntree: The main transverse beam of the body of a post mill pivoting on the top of main post.

Cullin Stones: Millstone imported from Cologne.

Curb: The circular timber or iron wall plate, supporting the revolving cap of a smock and tower mill.

Dagger Point: The second position for spreading a sail cloth on a common sail.

Damsel: An iron casting used with underdrift stones to assist the flow of grain to the stones.

Dead Curb: A curb which slips around on iron or brass pads on the cap frame without the use of rollers.

Dead Lead: The wide board replacing the shutters on the inner half of the leading edge of a double shuttered sail.

Double Shuttered Sail: A sail with shutters on both sides of the whip.

Drainage Mill: A windmill equipped for draining land with paddle wheels or pumps.

Dresser: A device used to separate flour out of meal consisting of a cylindrical wire sieve containing rotating brushes.

Dressing: Cutting the grinding surfaces of the millstones.

Driving Side: The trailing side of a sail.

Dust Floor: The top floor in a tower or smock mill beneath the cap.

Eye: The hole in the centre of the runner millstone or the inner third of the grinding surface of a millstone.

Eye Staff: A small staff used for testing the level around the eye of the stone.

Face Wheel: A gear wheel cogged on the face, used in conjunction with a pinion.

Fan: A wind wheel comprising a set of small vanes.

Fan Braces: Supports to the fan spars.

Fan Spars: The wooden uprights supporting the fan.

Fan Stage: The stage at the back of the cap giving access to the fantail of a tower or smock mill.

Fang Staff: East Anglian term for a brake lever.

Fantail: A fan set at the rear of the mill and at right angles to the sails, which provides the power for automatic winding gear that turns the mill into the 'eye of the wind'.

Felloe: The sections of the rim of a wooden wheel.

First Reef: The third of four positions for spreading the sail cloth of a common sail.

Flats: The thimbles in which the sail shutters are pivoted.

243

Floats: The paddles of the scoop wheel of a drainage mill.

Fly: See Fantail.

French Burr: A stone imported from France being built up of blocks of a freshwater quartz.

Full Sail: The last of four positions for spreading the sail cloth of a common sail.

Furrowing Strips: Timber strips used for marking out the furrows on a millstone.

Furrows: The main grooves cut in the grinding surface of a millstone.

Gallery: The platform around the cap of a tower or smock mill.

Gate: A slide sometimes used to control the flow of grain from the shoe to the stones.

Girts: The timbers running the full length of the side of a post mill, resting upon the crowntree and supporting the framing of the body of the mill.

Glutbox: The bearing used for disengaging a stone nut on a quant.

Governor: An automatic device to regulate the distance between the stones according to the speed of the wind.

Graft Shaft: An upright shaft which comprises both iron and wood.

Grease Wedge: The removable portion of the bearing round the neck of a stone spindle.

Great Spur Wheel: The main driving wheel mounted on the upright shaft which drives the stone nuts.

Grey Stones: See Peak Stones.

Gripe: Norfolk term for the brake.

Griped Arm: Norfolk term for a clasp arm.

Gudgeon: An iron pin projecting from a wooden shaft forming a bearing.

Hackle Plate: A square cover plate with leather washer that keeps dirt from entering the bearing of the stone spindle.

Harp: The segment of the grinding surface of a millstone which contains the lands and furrows.

Head Sick: A term describing a post mill when the body leans forward.

Hemlath: The longitudinal member at the outer edge of a sail frame which joins the ends of the sail bars.

Hollow Post Mill: A Dutch-type mill which is driven by an upright shaft taken down through the post to drive the machinery below.

Hoodway: Wooden casing enclosing the scoop wheel of a drainage mill.

Hopper: An open funnel-like wooden container supplying the grain to the millstones.

Horizontal Mill: A windmill powered by vanes or sails mounted on a vertical shaft.

Horse: The wooden frame supporting the hopper and shoe resting on the vat.

Hunting Cog: An odd cog introduced or omitted to prevent the same cogs meeting at every revolution and ensuring even wear.

Hurst: Heavy framework which supports underdrift millstone above the floor when the drive is on the same floor.

Jack: A tool used to check the vertical position of the stone spindle.

Jack-Ring: Iron frame for lifting the stone nut out of gear.

Jockey Pulley: A small pulley used to tension a belt.

Joggling Screen: A 'shaker' for sifting partly ground corn before a second grinding.

Keep: An iron or wooden block holding down the tail of a windshaft.

Keep Flange: A flange on the inner side of the curb under which the truck wheels run.

Lands: The flat raised surfaces between the furrows on the grinding face of a millstone.

Lantern Pinion: A gear consisting of a number of staves between two discs instead of cogs.

Leading Board: A narrow board fixed to the leading edge of a common or single shuttered sail.

Lighter Screw: The screw that passes through the bridge tree and is used to adjust it.

Listings: The webbing straps that connected the blinds of roller reefing sails.

Live Curb: A curb carrying the cap on rollers.

Luff: Turning the movable part of the mill so that the sails face the wind.

Mace Head: The head mounted on the tip end of a stone spindle driving and/or supporting the gimbal bar.

Main Post: The large upright timber post on top of which a post mill revolves.

Marsh Mill: See Drainage Mill.

Meal Bin: Bins to receive the meal from the stones.

Meal Floor: The floor with meal bins below the stone floor.

Meal Man: A man employed to separate the flour from the bran before bolters were used.

Meal Spout: A spout which conveys the meal from the stones to the meal bins.

Middling: A Kent term for the stock.

Millers Willow A wooden spring used to tension the shoe against the damsel or quant.

Millstone: The stones used to grind the grain comprising the bed and runner stone.

Neck Bearing: The main bearing of a windshaft, resting on a neck beam.

Neck of Stone Spindle: The upper journal of the stone spindle.

Neck of Windshaft: The front journal of the windshaft.

Neck Studs: The vertical timbers holding the neck bearing in place.

Overdrift Millstones: Stones driven from above.

Paddle: The metal plate fixed to the runner stone for sweeping the meal around the vat to the meal hole.

Paint Staff: A wooden staff used for marking the high spots when stone dressing.

Patent Sail: Shuttered sails with self-regulating control gear.

Peak Stone: A one-piece millstone quarried in the Derbyshire Peak.

Petticoat: The vertical weatherboarding extending downwards around the lower part of a cap to a smock or tower mill to prevent rain from being driven through the gap between the cap and body.

Pick: A pointed mill bill used for dressing stones.

Pinch Bar: A device used to lift the runner stone for dressing or renewal.

Pintle: The journal projecting from the top of the main post.

Pit Wheel: A driven gear mounted on the scoop wheel shaft.

Pointing Lines: The cords attached to sail cloths and used when reefing a common sail.

Poll End: The cast-iron double box with an opening at right angles at the end of the windshaft which the stocks are passed through and wedged.

Post: See Main Post.

Post Mill: A mill having a body mounted and turning on the main post.

Prick Post: The central vertical stud in the breast of a post mill.

Pritchell: A pointed chisel-like tool used with a hammer for dressing the furrows of a millstone.

Proof Staff: An iron staff for checking the working face of the paint staff when dressing stones.

Puncheons: The horizontal timbers bracing the cap circle to the sheers.

Quant: The iron spindle carrying the stone nut for driving an overdrift stone.

Quarterbars: Diagonal timbers of the substructure of a post mill from the ends of the horizontal crosstrees to the main post.

Quartering: The operation of turning the sails ninety degrees to the direction of the wind.

Quarter of a Smock Mill: One of the sides of a smock mill.

Rack: The gearing around the curb of a tower or smock mill.

Raddle: See Tiver.

Rap: A block of hard wood or bone on the shoe to take the knock of the quant or damsel.

Rigger: A device using chains or straps to disengage the stone nuts from the great spur wheel.

Rode Balk: See Breast Beam.

Roller Mill: A mill using metal rolls in place of the traditional stones.

Roller Reefing Sails: Sails using roller blinds instead of shutters.

Roundhouse: A building around the trestle of a post mill protecting the substructure and providing storage.

Rubbing Burr: A small piece of French burr used to rub down high spots when stone dressing.

Runner Stone: The upper revolving stone of a pair of millstone.

Rynd: A device let into the runner stone to take the drive before the mace and bar were introduced.

Sack Boy. A wooden bar with metal hooks for holding the mouth of a sack open.

Sack Chain: The chain used for hoisting sacks.

Sack Hoist: Device for hoisting sacks to the bin floor.

Sack Slide: A timber slide to one side of a ladder to a post mill for lowering sacks.

Sail Back: The strong whip of a sail used with a cross.

Sail Bars: The transverse members of a sail frame.

Sail Rods: See Shutter Bars.

Sails: The revolving arms of a mill which are turned by wind and so drives the machinery.

Samson Head: The iron castings fixed between the top of the post and the bottom of the crowntree to strengthen the pintle.

Scoop Wheel: The wheel with floats used to raise water to a high level on the marshes.

Scotch Wedge: A wooden block for raising a millstone.

Screener: A machine used for removing dust from grain prior to grinding.

Separator: A machine used in place of or in conjunction with a screener.

Sheaves: See Truck Wheels.

Sheers: The two longitudinal timbers from breast to tail under a body of a post mill; or the two timbers extending from front to back of cap.

Shoe: An inclined trough which feeds the grain from the hopper to the stones.

Shot Curb: A live curb on which a ring of rollers runs.

Shutter Bars: The rod the full length of the sail connecting together all the shutters on one side of a sail.

Shutters: The hinged vanes in spring or patent sails.

Sickle Dress: A stone dressed with curved furrows.

Single Shuttered Sail: A sail having shutters on the driving side only.

Skirt: The outer third of the grinding surface of a millstone.

Sky-scrapers: A Suffolk term for air brakes.

Slip Cogs: The removable cogs in a gear.

Slipper: See Shoe.

Smock Mill: A tower mill with a wooden tower instead of brick or stone.

Smutter: A vertical machine to remove smut from grain.

Spattle: A sliding shutter controlling the flow of grain from hopper to shoe.

Spider: A metal coupling fixed to the front end of the striking rod which operates the shutter bars; or the cast-iron frame for a wheel comprising hub and spokes.

Spill the Wind: A term meaning to open the shutters of a sail which was being driven.

Spindle Beam: The beam in a post mill that carries the top bearing of the upright shaft.

Sprattle Beam: A fixed horizontal beam carrying the upper bearing of the upright shaft.

Spring Sails: Sails with the shutters controlled by a spring.

Staff: See Paint Staff.

Stage: The platform round the body of a tower or smock mill.

Star Wheel: The iron centre into which the stocks carrying the vanes of a fantail are fitted.

Steelyard: A long iron lever linking the bridge tree or bray to the governors.

Stitching: See Cracking.

Stock: The main timbers which pass through the poll end to which the sails are fitted.

Stone Casing: See Vat.

Stone Dressing: The act of sharpening the stones.

Stone Floor: The floor on which the stones are situated.

Stone Nut: The final gear that drives the stones.

Stone Spindle: The spindle on which the runner stone is balanced.

Storm Hatch: A door above the neck of the windshaft to give access to the sails.

Striking Gear: The mechanism used to open and close the shutters of a patent sail or the blinds of a roller reefing sail.

Striking Rod: An iron rod that passes through the windshaft and actuates the striking gear in patent or roller reefing sails.

Stump Irons: These are bolted to the stocks to support the triangles of the striking gear.

Substructure: The main post, crosstrees and quarterbars supporting the body of a post mill.

Sunk Post Mill: A medieval post mill having its substructure buried below the surface of the ground.

Swallow: The relief of the grinding surface round the eye of the stone.

Sweep: A South of England term for a sail.

Sword Point: The first of four positions for spreading a sail cloth of a common sail.

Tail Beam: A beam supporting the tail bearing of the windshaft.

Tail Bearing: The bearing at the rear of the windshaft.

Tail Block: A block used when the tail beam is dispensed with.

Tail of a Mill: The rear end of a post mill from the main post.

Tail Pole: The timber lever attached to the tail of a post mill or to a cap on a tower or smock mill for winding a mill by hand.

Tail Wheel: A wheel smaller than the brake wheel mounted on the tail of the windshaft to drive the stones in the rear of a post mill.

Tail-winding: A wind that catches the sails from the rear.

Talthur: The lever pivoted on the side of the tail pole used to raise the ladder of a post mill clear of the ground prior to winding the mill.

Temse: A sieve used in bolting meal by hand.

Tentering Gear: The device for making fine adjustments to the gap between millstones.

Thrift: The wooden handle usually of ash into which mill bill or picks were held and wedged.

Thrust Block: A block that carried the thrust bearing of the windshaft.

Tiver: A mixture of red oxide and fat or water used on a wooden staff for finding the high spots when stone dressing.

Toll: A portion of meal formerly taken by the miller for payment for grinding corn or dressing meal.

Tower Mill: A windmill with a tower of brick, masonry or other material.

Trail Stick: A lever operating a bell alarm.

Trammel: A wooden gauge used to check the plumbing of the stone spindle.

Trestle: The substructure of a post mill.

Triangles: Iron cranks operating the front striking gear of patent sails.

Truck Wheel: Iron wheels fixed to the underside of the cap frame and running on the inside face of the curb to centre the cap.

Trundle Wheel: A wheel having wooden pegs projecting from the face instead of cogs.

Tun: See Vat.

Twist Peg: A wooden peg to which the cord that controls the flow of grain from the shoe into the eye of the stone is attached.

Underdrift Millstones: Stones driven from beneath.

Uplong: The intermediate longitudinal member of a sail frame.

Upright Shaft: The main driving shaft of the mill on which the wallower and great spur wheel is mounted.

Vanes: The shutters in spring and patent sails and also the blades of a fantail.

Vat: Removable circular or octagonal wooden case enclosing the millstones.

Wallower: Large horizontal wheel receiving its drive directly from the brake wheel and with indirect drive to the stones.

Weather: See Angle of Weather.

Weather-beam: See Breast Beam.

Whip: The main timber of a sail bolted to the stock.

Winding: The process of turning the mill sails into the eye of the wind.

Windshaft: The main axle of iron or wood that carries the sails and the brake wheel.

Winnower: A fan which blows dust, etc. from the grain as it descends a chute.

Wire Machine: See Dresser.

Worm: A cylindrical gear with a helical thread and used with a rack in the winding gear.

Y-wheel: A wooden or iron wheel which has metal 'Y's round the circumference to carry a chain or rope so increasing the grip.

Yoke: Two wooden bars fixed to the tail pole against which the miller pushes a post mill into the wind.

Bibliography

BATTEN, M. I., *English Windmills Vol I* (Architectural Press 1930)

BENNETT & ELTON, *History of Corn Milling Vol II* (Simpkin Marshall)

CLARKE, Allen, *Windmill Land* (W. Foulsham 1933)——, *Blackpool Walks & Rides* (Teddy Ashton Publishing Co. 1920)

DE LITTLE, R. J., *The Windmill Yesterday & Today* (John Baker 1972)

FARRIES, K. G. & MASON, M. T., *The Windmills of Surrey & Inner London* (Charles Skilton 1966)

FINCH, W. Coles, *Watermills & Windmills* (C. W. Daniel 1933)

FREESE, Stanley, *Windmills & Millwrighting* (Cambridge University Press 1957)

HEMMING, Rev. Peter, *Windmills in Sussex* (C. W. Daniel 1936)

HOPKINS, R. Thurston, *Old Watermills & Windmills* (Philip Allan *c.* 1930)

HOPKINS, R. Thurston & FREESE, Stanley, *In Search of English Windmills* (Cecil Palmer 1931)

MAIS, S. P. B., *England of the Windmills* (J. M. Dent 1931)

REYNOLDS, John, *Windmills & Watermills* (Hugh Evelyn Ltd 1970)

SKILTON, C. P., *British Windmills & Watermills* (Collins 1947)

SMITH, Donald, *English Windmills Vol II* (Architectural Press 1932)

VINCE, J. N. T., *Discovering Windmills* (Shire Publications 1969)

WAILES, Rex, *Windmills in England* (Architectural Press 1948)

——, *The English Windmill* (Routledge & Kegan Paul 1954)

WEST, Jenny, *The Windmills of Kent* (Charles Skilton 1974)

INDEX

621.4 Brown, R. J.
B
      Windmills of England

DATE			